Night

with Related Readings

Glencoe
McGraw-Hill

New York, New York Columbus, Ohio Woodland Hills, California Peoria, Illinois

Acknowledgments

Grateful acknowledgment is given authors, publishers, photographers, museums, and agents for permission to reprint the following copyrighted material. Every effort has been made to determine copyright owners. In case of any omissions, the Publisher will be pleased to make suitable acknowledgments in future editions.

NIGHT by Elie Wiesel, translated by Stella Rodway. Translation copyright © 1960 by MacGibbon and Kee. Translation copyright renewed © 1988 by The Collins Publishing Group. All rights reserved. Published by arrangement with Hill and Wang, a division of Farrar, Straus & Giroux, Inc.

From "A Wound That Will Never Be Healed: An Interview with Elie Wiesel," by Bob Costas, is from Telling the Tale: A Tribute to Elie Wiesel on the Occasion of His 65th Birthday, ed. by Harry James Cargas. Copyright © 1993 by Time Being Press, Inc. All rights reserved. Reprinted by permission of Time Being Books.

Text excerpt, "Cattle Car Complex" from ELIJAH VISIBLE, by Thane Rosenbaum. Copyright © 1996 St. Martin's Press, pp. 3–11. Reprinted by permission of St. Martin's Press.

Assault on History and Rewriting History 101: Bradley Smith's Campus Campaign by Bob Keeler. Reprinted with permission © Newsday, Inc. 1994.

From SONG OF SURVIVAL, WOMEN INTERNED, by Helen Colijn, copyright © 1995, White Cloud Press, pp. 95–106. Reprinted by permission of White Cloud Press.

Poems from I NEVER SAW ANOTHER BUTTERFLY by Hana Volavková (editor). Copyright © 1978, 1993 by Artia, Prague. Compilation copyright © by Schocken Books, Inc. Reprinted by permission of Schocken Books, distributed by Pantheon Books, a division of Random House, Inc.

Room with a Bunkbed by Ericka Taussigová, Figure of Little Girls by Jana Hellerová, Man with a Mustache by Hanuš Klauber, Bird and Butterfly (Artist Unknown), Untitled drawing by Helena Schanzerová, Man on Boat by Elly Hellerová, Garden by Ruth Čechová. Drawings reprinted by permission of The Jewish Museum in Prague/United States Holocaust Memorial Museum.

Cover Art: Freshman Brown/SuperStock

Contents

Continued

Contents Continued

Night

❧

Elie Wiesel

Translation by Stella Rodway

In memory of my parents

and of my little sister,

Tzipora

One

THEY CALLED HIM Moché the Beadle, as though he had never had a sur-name in his life. He was a man of all work at a Hasidic synagogue. The Jews of Sighet—that little town in Transylvania where I spent my childhood—were very fond of him. He was very poor and lived humbly. Generally my fellow townspeople, though they would help the poor, were not particularly fond of them. Moché the Beadle was the exception. Nobody ever felt em-barrassed by him. Nobody ever felt encumbered by his presence. He was a past master in the art of making himself insignificant, of seeming invisible.

Physically he was as awkward as a clown. He made people smile, with his waiflike timidity. I loved his great, dreaming eyes, their gaze lost in the dis-tance. He spoke little. He used to sing, or, rather, to chant. Such snatches as you could hear told of the suffering of the divinity, of the Exile of Providence, who, according to the cabbala, awaits his deliverance in that of man.

I got to know him toward the end of 1941. I was twelve. I believed pro-foundly. During the day I studied the Talmud, and at night I ran to the syna-gogue to weep over the destruction of the Temple.

One day I asked my father to find me a master to guide me in my studies of the cabbala.

"You're too young for that. Maimonides said it was only at thirty that one had the right to venture into the perilous world of mysticism. You must first study the basic subjects within your own understanding."

My father was a cultured, rather unsentimental man. There was never any display of emotion, even at home. He was more concerned with others than with his own family. The Jewish community in Sighet held him in the great-est esteem. They often used to consult him about public matters and even about private ones. There were four of us children: Hilda, the eldest; then Béa; I was the third, and the only son; the baby of the family was Tzipora.

My parents ran a shop. Hilda and Béa helped them with the work. As for me, they said my place was at school.

"There aren't any cabbalists at Sighet," my father would repeat.

He wanted to drive the notion out of my head. But it was in vain.
I found a master for myself, Moché the Beadle.

He had noticed me one day at dusk, when I was praying.

"Why do you weep when you pray?" he asked me, as though he had known me a long time.

"I don't know why," I answered, greatly disturbed.

The question had never entered my head. I wept because—because of something inside me that felt the need for tears. That was all I knew.

"Why do you pray?" he asked me, after a moment.

Why did I pray? A strange question. Why did I live? Why did I breathe?

"I don't know why," I said, even more disturbed and ill at ease. "I don't know why."

After that day I saw him often. He explained to me with great insistence that every question possessed a power that did not lie in the answer.

"Man raises himself toward God by the questions he asks Him," he was fond of repeating. "That is the true dialogue. Man questions God and God answers. But we don't understand His answers. We can't understand them. Because they come from the depths of the soul, and they stay there until death. You will find the true answers, Eliezer, only within yourself!"

"And why do you pray, Moché?" I asked him.

"I pray to the God within me that He will give me the strength to ask Him the right questions."

We talked like this nearly every evening. We used to stay in the synagogue after all the faithful had left, sitting in the gloom, where a few half-burned candles still gave a flickering light.

One evening I told him how unhappy I was because I could not find a master in Sighet to instruct me in the Zohar, the cabbalistic books, the secrets of Jewish mysticism. He smiled indulgently. After a long silence, he said:

"There are a thousand and one gates leading into the orchard of mystical truth. Every human being has his own gate. We must never make the mistake of wanting to enter the orchard by any gate but our own. To do this is dangerous for the one who enters and also for those who are already there."

And Moché the Beadle, the poor barefoot of Sighet, talked to me for long hours of the revelations and mysteries of the cabbala. It was with him that my initiation began. We would read together, ten times over, the same page of the Zohar. Not to learn it by heart, but to extract the divine essence from it.

And throughout those evenings a conviction grew in me that Moché the Beadle would draw me with him into eternity, into that time where question and answer would become *one*.

Then one day they expelled all the foreign Jews from Sighet. And Moché the Beadle was a foreigner.

Crammed into cattle trains by Hungarian police, they wept bitterly. We stood on the platform and wept too. The train disappeared on the horizon; it left nothing behind but its thick, dirty smoke.

I heard a Jew behind me heave a sigh.

"What can we expect?" he said. "It's war. . . ."

The deportees were soon forgotten. A few days after they had gone, people were saying that they had arrived in Galicia, were working there, and were even satisfied with their lot.

Several days passed. Several weeks. Several months. Life had returned to normal. A wind of calmness and reassurance blew through our houses. The traders were doing good business, the students lived buried in their books, and the children played in the streets.

One day, as I was just going into the synagogue, I saw, sitting on a bench near the door, Moché the Beadle.

He told his story and that of his companions. The train full of deportees had crossed the Hungarian frontier and on Polish territory had been taken in charge by the Gestapo. There it had stopped. The Jews had to get out and climb into lorries. The lorries drove toward a forest. The Jews were made to get out. They were made to dig huge graves. And when they had finished their work, the Gestapo began theirs. Without passion, without haste, they slaughtered their prisoners. Each one had to go up to the hole and present his neck. Babies were thrown into the air and the machine gunners used them as targets. This was in the forest of Galicia, near Kolomaye. How had Moché the Beadle escaped? Miraculously. He was wounded in the leg and taken for dead. . . .

Through long days and nights, he went from one Jewish house to another, telling the story of Malka, the young girl who had taken three days to die, and of Tobias, the tailor, who had begged to be killed before his sons. . . .

Moché had changed. There was no longer any joy in his eyes. He no longer sang. He no longer talked to me of God or the cabbala, but only of what he had seen. People refused not only to believe his stories, but even to listen to them.

"He's just trying to make us pity him. What an imagination he has!" they said. Or even: "Poor fellow. He's gone mad."

And as for Moché, he wept.

"Jews, listen to me. It's all I ask of you. I don't want money or pity. Only listen to me," he would cry between prayers at dusk and the evening prayers.

I did not believe him myself. I would often sit with him in the evening after the service, listening to his stories and trying my hardest to understand his grief. I felt only pity for him.

"They take me for a madman," he would whisper, and tears, like drops of wax, flowed from his eyes.

Once, I asked him this question:

"Why are you so anxious that people should believe what you say. In your place, I shouldn't care whether they believed me or not. . . ."

He closed his eyes, as though to escape time.

"You don't understand," he said in despair. "You can't understand. I have been saved miraculously. I managed to get back here. Where did I get the strength from? I wanted to come back to Sighet to tell you the story of my death. So that you could prepare yourselves while there was still time. To live? I don't attach my importance to my life any more. I'm alone. No, I wanted to come back, and to warn you. And see how it is, no one will listen to me. . . ."

That was toward the end of 1942. Afterward life returned to normal. The London radio, which we listened to every evening, gave us heartening news: the daily bombardment of Germany; Stalingrad; preparation for the second front. And we, the Jews of Sighet, were waiting for better days, which would not be long in coming now.

I continued to devote myself to my studies. By day, the Talmud, at night, the cabbala. My father was occupied with his business and the doings of the community. My grandfather had come to celebrate the New Year with us, so that he could attend the services of the famous rabbi of Borsche. My mother began to think that it was high time to find a suitable young man for Hilda.

Thus the year 1943 passed by.

Spring 1944. Good news from the Russian front. No doubt could remain now of Germany's defeat. It was only a question of time—of months or weeks perhaps.

The trees were in blossom. This was a year like any other, with its springtime, its betrothals, its weddings and births.

People said: "The Russian army's making gigantic strides forward . . . Hitler won't be able to do us any harm, even if he wants to."

Yes, we even doubted that he wanted to exterminate us.

Was he going to wipe out a whole people? Could he exterminate a population scattered throughout so many countries? So many millions! What methods could he use? And in the middle of the twentieth century!

Besides, people were interested in everything—in strategy, in diplomacy, in politics, in Zionism—but not in their own fate.

Even Moché the Beadle was silent. He was weary of speaking. He wandered in the synagogue or in the streets, with his eyes down, his back bent, avoiding people's eyes.

At that time, it was still possible to obtain emigration permits for Palestine. I had asked my father to sell out, liquidate his business, and leave.

"I'm too old, my son," he replied. "I'm too old to start a new life. I'm too old to start from scratch again in a country so far away. . . ."

The Budapest radio announced that the Fascist party had come into power. Horthy had been forced to ask one of the leaders of the Nyilas party to form a new government.

Still this was not enough to worry us. Of course we had heard about the Fascists, but they were still just an abstraction to us. This was only a change in the administration.

The following day, there was more disturbing news: with government permission, German troops had entered Hungarian territory.

Here and there, anxiety was aroused. One of our friends, Berkovitz, who had just returned from the capital, told us:

"The Jews in Budapest are living in an atmosphere of fear and terror. There are anti-Semitic incidents every day, in the streets, in the trains. The Fascists are attacking Jewish shops and synagogues. The situation is getting very serious."

This news spread like wildfire through Sighet. Soon it was on everyone's lips. But not for long. Optimism soon revived.

"The Germans won't get as far as this. They'll stay in Budapest. There are strategic and political reasons. . . ."

Before three days had passed, German army cars had appeared in our streets.

Anguish. German soldiers—with their steel helmets, and their emblem, the death's head.

However, our first impressions of the Germans were most reassuring. The officers were billeted in private houses, even in the homes of Jews. Their attitude toward their hosts was distant, but polite. They never demanded the impossible, made no unpleasant comments, and even smiled occasionally at the mistress of the house. One German officer lived in the house opposite ours. He had a room with the Kahn family. They said he was a charming man—calm, likable, polite, and sympathetic. Three days after he moved in he brought Madame Kahn a box of chocolates. The optimists rejoiced.

"Well, there you are, you see! What did we tell you? You wouldn't believe us. There they are your Germans! What do you think of them? Where is their famous cruelty?"

The Germans were already in the town, the Fascists were already in power, the verdict had already been pronounced, yet the Jews of Sighet continued to smile.

The week of Passover. The weather was wonderful. My mother bustled round her kitchen. There were no longer any synagogues open. We gathered in private houses: the Germans were not to be provoked. Practically every rabbi's flat became a house of prayer.

We drank, we ate, we sang. The Bible bade us rejoice during the seven days of the feast, to be happy. But our hearts were not in it. Our hearts had been beating more rapidly for some days. We wished the feast were over, so that we should not have to play this comedy any longer.

On the seventh day of Passover the curtain rose. The Germans arrested the leaders of the Jewish community.

From that moment, everything happened very quickly. The race toward death had begun.

The first step: Jews would not be allowed to leave their houses for three days—on pain of death.

Moché the Beadle came running to our house.

"I warned you," he cried to my father. And, without waiting for a reply, he fled.

That same day the Hungarian police burst into all the Jewish houses in the street. A Jew no longer had the right to keep in his house gold, jewels, or any objects of value. Everything had to be handed over to the authorities—on pain of death. My father went down into the cellar and buried our savings.

At home, my mother continued to busy herself with her usual tasks. At times she would pause and gaze at us, silent.

When the three days were up, there was a new decree: every Jew must wear the yellow star.

Some of the prominent members of the community came to see my father—who had highly placed connections in the Hungarian police—to ask him what he thought of the situation. My father did not consider it so grim—but perhaps he did not want to dishearten the others or rub salt in their wounds:

"The yellow star? Oh well, what of it? You don't die of it. . . ."

(Poor Father! Of what then did you die?)

But already they were issuing new decrees. We were no longer allowed to go into restaurants or cafes, to travel on the railway, to attend the synagogue, to go out into the street after six o'clock.

Then came the ghetto.

Two ghettos were set up in Sighet. A large one, in the center of the town, occupied four streets, and another smaller one extended over several small side streets in the outlying district. The street where we lived, Serpent Street, was inside the first ghetto. We still lived, therefore, in our own house. But as it was at the corner, the windows facing the outside street had to be blocked up. We gave up some of our rooms to relatives who had been driven out of their flats.

Little by little life returned to normal. The barbed wire which fenced us in did not cause us any real fear. We even thought ourselves rather well off; we were entirely self-contained. A little Jewish republic. . . . We appointed a Jewish Council, a Jewish police, an office for social assistance, a labor committee, a hygiene department—a whole government machinery.

Everyone marveled at it. We should no longer have before our eyes those hostile faces, those hate-laden stares. Our fear and anguish were at an end. We were living among Jews, among brothers. . . .

Of course, there were still some unpleasant moments. Every day the Germans came to fetch men to stoke coal on the military trains. There were not many volunteers for work of this kind. But apart from that the atmosphere was peaceful and reassuring.

The general opinion was that we were going to remain in the ghetto until the end of the war, until the arrival of the Red Army. Then everything would be as before. It was neither German nor Jew who ruled the ghetto—it was illusion.

On the Saturday before Pentecost, in the spring sunshine, people strolled, carefree and unheeding, through the swarming streets. They chatted happily. The children played games on the pavements. With some of my schoolmates, I sat in the Ezra Malik gardens, studying a treatise on the Talmud.

Night fell. There were twenty people gathered in our back yard. My father was telling them anecdotes and expounding his own views on the situation. He was a good story teller.

Suddenly the gate opened and Stern—a former tradesman who had become a policeman—came in and took my father aside. Despite the gathering dusk, I saw my father turn pale.

"What's the matter?" we all asked him.

"I don't know. I've been summoned to an extraordinary meeting of the council. Something must have happened."

The good story he had been in the middle of telling us was to remain unfinished.

"I'm going there," he went on. "I shall be back as soon as I can. I'll tell you all about it. Wait for me."

We were prepared to wait for some hours. The back yard became like the hall outside an operating room. We were only waiting for the door to open—to see the opening of the firmament itself. Other neighbors, having heard rumors, had come to join us. People looked at their watches. The time passed very slowly. What could such a long meeting mean?

"I've got a premonition of evil," said my mother. "This afternoon I noticed some new faces in the ghetto—two German officers, from the Gestapo, I believe. Since we've been here, not a single officer has ever shown himself. . . ."

It was nearly midnight. No one had wanted to go to bed. A few people had paid a flying visit to their homes to see that everything was all right. Others had returned home, but they left instructions that they were to be told as soon as my father came back.

At last the door opened and he appeared. He was pale. At once he was surrounded.

"What happened? Tell us what happened! Say something!"

How avid we were at that moment for one word of confidence, one sentence to say that there were no grounds for fear, that the meeting could not have been more commonplace, more routine, that it had only been a question of social welfare, of sanitary arrangements! But one glance at my father's haggard face was enough.

"I have terrible news," he said at last. "Deportation."

The ghetto was to be completely wiped out. We were to leave street by street, starting the following day.

We wanted to know everything, all the details. The news had stunned everyone, yet we wanted to drain the bitter draft to the dregs.

"Where are we being taken?"

This was a secret. A secret from all except one: the President of the Jewish Council. But he would not say; he *could* not say. The Gestapo had threatened to shoot him if he talked.

"There are rumors going around," said my father in a broken voice, "that we're going somewhere in Hungary, to work in the brick factories. Apparently, the reason is that the front is too close here. . . ."

And, after a moment's silence, he added:

"Each person will be allowed to take only his own personal belongings. A bag on our backs, some food, a few clothes. Nothing else."

Again a heavy silence.

"Go and wake the neighbors up," said my father. "So that they can get ready."

The shadows beside me awoke as from a long sleep. They fled, silently, in all directions.

For a moment we were alone. Then suddenly Batia Reich, a relative who was living with us, came into the room:

"There's someone knocking on the blocked-up window, the one that faces outside.!"

It was not until after the war that I learned who it was that had knocked. It was an inspector in the Hungarian police, a friend of my father. Before we went into the ghetto, he had said to us: "Don't worry. If you're in any danger, I'll warn you." If he could have spoken to us that evening, we could perhaps have fled. . . . But by the time we had managed to open the window, it was too late. There was no one outside.

The ghetto awoke. One by one, lights came on in the windows.

I went into the house of one of my father's friends. I woke up the head of the household, an old man with a gray beard and the eyes of a dreamer. He was stooped from long nights of study.

"Get up, sir, get up! You've got to get ready for the journey! You're going to be expelled from here tomorrow with your whole family, and all the rest of the Jews. Where to? Don't ask me, sir. Don't ask me any questions. Only God could answer you. For heaven's sake, get up."

He had not understood a word of what I was saying. He probably thought I had gone out of my mind.

"What tale is this? Get ready for the journey? What journey? Why? What's going on? Have you gone mad?"

Still half asleep, he stared at me with terror-stricken eyes, as though he expected me to burst out laughing and say in the end, "Get back to bed. Go to sleep. Pleasant dreams. Nothing's happened at all. It was just a joke."

My throat was dry, the words choked in it, paralyzing my lips. I could not say any more.

Then he understood. He got out of bed and with automatic movements began to get dressed. Then he went up to the bed where his wife slept and touched her brow with infinite tenderness; she opened her eyes, and it seemed to me that her lips were brushed by a smile. Then he went to his children's beds and woke them swiftly, dragging them from their dreams. I fled.

Time passed very quickly. It was already four o'clock in the morning. My father ran to right and left, exhausted, comforting friends, running to the Jewish Council to see if the edict had not been revoked in the meantime. To the very last moment, a germ of hope stayed alive in our hearts.

The women were cooking eggs, roasting meat, baking cakes, and making knapsacks. The children wandered all over the place, hanging their heads, not knowing what to do with themselves, where to go, to keep from getting in the way of the grown-ups. Our back yard had become a real market place. Household treasures, valuable carpets, silver candelabra, prayer books, Bibles, and other religious articles littered the dusty ground beneath a wonderfully blue sky; pathetic objects which looked as though they had never belonged to anyone.

By eight o'clock in the morning, a weariness like molten lead began to settle in the veins, the limbs, the brain. I was in the midst of my prayers when suddenly there were shouts in the street. I tore myself from my phylacteries and ran to the window. Hungarian police had entered the ghetto and were shouting in the neighboring street:

"All Jews outside! Hurry!"

Some Jewish police went into the houses, saying in broken voices:

"The time's come now . . . you've got to leave all this. . . ."

The Hungarian police struck out with truncheons and rifle butts, to right and left, without reason, indiscriminately, their blows falling upon old men and women, children and invalids alike.

One by one the houses emptied, and the street filled with people and bundles. By ten o'clock, all the condemned were outside. The police took a roll call, once, twice, twenty times. The heat was intense. Sweat streamed from faces and bodies.

Children cried for water.

Water? There was plenty, close at hand, in the houses, in the yards, but they were forbidden to break the ranks.

"Water! Mummy! Water!"

The Jewish police from the ghetto were able to go and fill a few jugs secretly. Since my sisters and I were destined for the last convoy and we were still allowed to move about, we helped them as well as we could.

Then, at last, at one o'clock in the afternoon, came the signal to leave.

There was joy—yes, joy. Perhaps they thought that God could have devised no torment in hell worse than that of sitting there among the bundles, in the middle of the road, beneath a blazing sun; that anything would be preferable to that. They began their journey without a backward glance at the abandoned streets, the dead, empty houses, the gardens, the tombstones. . . . On everyone's back was a pack. In everyone's eyes was suffering drowned in tears. Slowly, heavily, the procession made its way to the gate of the ghetto.

And there was I, on the pavement, unable to make a move. Here came the Rabbi, his back bent, his face shaved, his pack on his back. His mere presence among the deportees added a touch of unreality to the scene. It was like a page torn from some story book, from some historical novel about the captivity of Babylon or the Spanish Inquisition.

One by one they passed in front of me, teachers, friends, others, all those I had been afraid of, all those I once could have laughed at, all those I had lived with over the years. They went by, fallen, dragging their packs, dragging their lives, deserting their homes, the years of their childhood, cringing like beaten dogs.

They passed without a glance in my direction. They must have envied me.

The procession disappeared round the corner of the street. A few paces farther on, and they would have passed beyond the ghetto walls.

The street was like a market place that had suddenly been abandoned. Everything could be found there: suitcases, portfolios, briefcases, knives, plates, banknotes, papers, faded portraits. All those things that people had thought of taking with them, and which in the end they had left behind. They had lost all value.

Everywhere rooms lay open. Doors and windows gaped onto the emptiness. Everything was free for anyone, belonging to nobody. It was simply a matter of helping oneself. An open tomb.

A hot summer sun.

We had spent the day fasting. But we were not very hungry. We were exhausted.

My father had accompanied the deportees as far as the entrance of the ghetto. They first had to go through the big synagogue, where they were minutely searched, to see that they were not taking away any gold, silver, or other objects of value. There were outbreaks of hysteria and blows with the truncheons.

"When is our turn coming?" I asked my father.

"The day after tomorrow. At least—at least, unless things turn out differently. A miracle, perhaps. . . ."

Where were the people being taken to? Didn't anyone know yet? No, the secret was well kept.

Night had fallen. That evening we went to bed early. My father said:

"Sleep well, children. It's not until the day after tomorrow, Tuesday."

Monday passed like a small summer cloud, like a dream in the first daylight hours.

Busy with getting our packs ready, with baking bread and cakes, we no longer thought of anything. The verdict had been delivered.

That evening, our mother made us go to bed very early, to conserve our strength, she said. It was our last night at home.

I was up at dawn. I wanted time to pray before we were expelled.

My father had got up earlier to go and seek information. He came back at about eight o'clock. Good news: it wasn't today that we were leaving the town. We were only to move into the little ghetto. There we would wait for the last transport. We should be the last to leave.

At nine o'clock, Sunday's scenes began all over again. Policemen with truncheons yelling:

"All Jews outside!"

We were ready. I was the first to leave. I did not want to see my parents' faces. I did not want to break into tears. We stayed sitting down in the middle of the road, as the others had done the day before yesterday. There was the same infernal heat. The same thirst. But there was no longer anyone left to bring us water.

I looked at our house, where I had spent so many years in my search for God; in fasting in order to hasten the coming of the Messiah; in imagining what my life would be like. Yet I felt little sorrow. I thought of nothing.

"Get up! Count off!"

Standing. Counting off. Sitting down. Standing up again. On the ground once more. Endlessly. We waited impatiently to be fetched. What were they waiting for? At last the order came:

"Forward march!"

My father wept. It was the first time I had ever seen him weep. I had never imagined that he could. As for my mother, she walked with a set expression on her face, without a word, deep in thought. I looked at my little sister Tzipora, her fair hair well combed, a red coat over her arm, a little girl of seven. The bundle on her back was too heavy for her. She gritted her teeth. She knew by now that it would be useless to complain. The police were striking out with their truncheons. "Faster!" I had no strength left. The journey had only just begun, and I felt so weak. . . .

"Faster! Faster! Get on with you, lazy swine!" yelled the Hungarian police.

It was from that moment that I began to hate them, and my hate is still the only link between us today. They were our first oppressors. They were the first of the faces of hell and death.

We were ordered to run. We advanced in double time. Who would have thought we were so strong? Behind their windows, behind their shutters, our compatriots looked out at us as we passed.

At last we reached our destination. Throwing our bags to the ground, we sank down:

"Oh God, Lord of the Universe, take pity upon us in Thy great mercy. . . ."

The little ghetto. Three days before, people had still been living there—the people who owned the things we were using now. They had been expelled. Already we had completely forgotten them.

The disorder was greater than in the big ghetto. The people must have been driven out unexpectedly. I went to see the rooms where my uncle's family had lived. On the table there was a half-finished bowl of soup. There was a pie waiting to be put in the oven. Books were littered about on the floor. Perhaps my uncle had had dreams of taking them with him?

We settled in. (What a word!) I went to get some wood; my sisters lit the fire. Despite her own weariness, my mother began to prepare a meal.

"We must keep going, we must keep going," she kept on repeating.

The people's morale was not too bad; we were beginning to get used to the situation. In the street, they even went so far as to have optimistic conversations. The Boche would not have time to expel us, they were saying . . . as far as those who had already been deported were concerned, it was too bad; no more could be done. But they would probably allow us to live out our wretched little lives here, until the end of the war.

The ghetto was not guarded. Everyone could come and go as they pleased. Our old servant, Martha, came to see us. Weeping bitterly, she begged us to come to her village, where she could give us a safe refuge. My father did not want to hear of it.

"You can go if you want to," he said to me and to my older sisters. "I shall stay here with your mother and the child. . . ."

Naturally, we refused to be separated.

Night. No one prayed, so that the night would pass quickly. The stars were only sparks of the fire which devoured us. Should that fire die out one day, there would be nothing left in the sky but dead stars, dead eyes.

There was nothing else to do but to get into bed, into the beds of the absent ones; to rest, to gather one's strength.

At dawn, there was nothing left of this melancholy. We felt as though we were on holiday. People were saying:

"Who knows? Perhaps we are being deported for our own good. The front isn't very far off; we shall soon be able to hear the guns. And then the civilian population would be evacuated anyway. . . ."

"Perhaps they were afraid we might help the guerrillas. . . ."

"If you ask me, the whole business of deportation is just a farce. Oh yes, don't laugh. The Boches just want to steal our jewelry. They know we've buried everything, and that they'll have to hunt for it: it's easier when the owners are on holiday. . . ."

On holiday!

These optimistic speeches, which no one believed, helped to pass the time. The few days we lived here went by pleasantly enough, in peace. People were better disposed toward one another. There were no longer any questions of wealth, of social distinction, and importance, only people all condemned to the same fate—still unknown.

Saturday, the day of rest, was chosen for our expulsion.

The night before, we had the traditional Friday evening meal. We said the customary grace for the bread and wine and swallowed our food without a word. We were, we felt, gathered for the last time round the family table. I spent the night turning over thoughts and memories in my mind, unable to find sleep.

At dawn, we were in the street, ready to leave. This time there were no Hungarian police. An agreement had been made with the Jewish Council that they should organize it all themselves.

Our convoy went toward the main synagogue. The town seemed deserted. Yet our friends of yesterday were probably waiting behind their shutters for the moment when they could pillage our houses.

The synagogue was like a huge station: luggage and tears. The altar was broken, the hangings torn down, the walls bare. There were so many of us that we could scarcely breathe. We spent a horrible twenty-four hours there. There were men downstairs; women on the first floor. It was Saturday; it was as though we had come to attend the service. Since no one could go out, people were relieving themselves in a corner.

The following morning, we marched to the station, where a convoy of cattle wagons was waiting. The Hungarian police made us get in—eighty people in each car. We were left a few loaves of bread and some buckets of water. The bars at the window were checked, to see that they were not loose. Then the cars were sealed. In each car one person was placed in charge. If anyone escaped, he would be shot.

Two Gestapo officers strolled about on the platform, smiling: all things considered, everything had gone off very well.

A prolonged whistle split the air. The wheels began to grind. We were on our way.

Two

LYING DOWN WAS out of the question, and we were only able to sit by deciding to take turns. There was very little air. The lucky ones who happened to be near a window could see the blossoming countryside roll by.

After two days of traveling, we began to be tortured by thirst. Then the heat became unbearable.

Free from all social constraint, the young people gave way openly to instinct, taking advantage of the darkness to copulate in our midst, without caring about anyone else, as though they were alone in the world. The rest pretended not to notice anything.

We still had a few provisions left. But we never ate enough to satisfy our hunger. To save was our rule; to save up for tomorrow. Tomorrow might be worse.

The train stopped at Kaschau, a little town on the Czechoslovak frontier. We realized then that we were not going to stay in Hungary. Our eyes were opened, but too late.

The door of the car slid open. A German officer, accompanied by a Hungarian lieutenant-interpreter, came up and introduced himself.

"From this moment, you come under the authority of the German army. Those of you who still have gold, silver, or watches in your possession must give them up now. Anyone who is later found to have kept anything will be shot on the spot. Secondly, anyone who feels ill may go to the hospital car. That's all."

The Hungarian lieutenant went among us with a basket and collected the last possessions from those who no longer wished to taste the bitterness of terror.

"There are eighty of you in the wagon," added the German officer." If anyone is missing, you'll all be shot, like dogs. . . ."

They disappeared. The doors were closed. We were caught in a trap, right up to our necks. The doors were nailed up; the way back was finally cut off. The world was a cattle wagon hermetically sealed.

We had a woman with us named Madame Schachter. She was about fifty; her ten-year-old son was with her, crouched in a corner. Her husband and two eldest sons had been deported with the first transport by mistake. The separation had completely broken her.

I knew her well. A quiet woman with tense, burning eyes, she had often been to our house. Her husband, who was a pious man, spent his days and nights in study, and it was she who worked to support the family.

Madame Schachter had gone out of her mind. On the first day of the journey she had already begun to moan and to keep asking why she had been separated from her family. As time went on, her cries grew hysterical.

On the third night, while we slept, some of us sitting one against the other and some standing, a piercing cry split the silence:

"Fire! I can see a fire! I can see a fire!"

There was a moment's panic. Who was it who had cried out? It was Madame Schachter. Standing in the middle of the wagon, in the pale light from the windows, she looked like a withered tree in a cornfield. She pointed her arm toward the window, screaming:

"Look! Look at it! Fire! A terrible fire! Mercy! *Oh, that fire!*"

Some of the men pressed up against the bars. There was nothing there; only the darkness.

The shock of this terrible awakening stayed with us for a long time. We still trembled from it. With every groan of the wheels on the rail, we felt that an abyss was about to open beneath our bodies. Powerless to still our own anguish, we tried to console ourselves:

"She's mad, poor soul. . . ."

Someone had put a damp cloth on her brow, to calm her, but still her screams went on:

"Fire! Fire!"

Her little boy was crying, hanging onto her skirt, trying to take hold of her hands. "It's all right, Mummy! There's nothing there. . . . Sit down. . . ." This shook me even more than his mother's screams had done.

Some women tried to calm her. "You'll find your husband and your sons again . . . in a few days. . . ."

She continued to scream, breathless, her voice broken by sobs. "Jews, listen to me! I can see a fire! There are huge flames! It is a furnace!"

It was as though she were possessed by an evil spirit which spoke from the depths of her being.

We tried to explain it away, more to calm ourselves and to recover our own breath than to comfort her. "She must be very thirsty, poor thing! That's why she keeps talking about a fire devouring her."

But it was in vain. Our terror was about to burst the sides of the train. Our nerves were at breaking point. Our flesh was creeping. It was as though madness were taking possession of us all. We could stand it no longer. Some of the young men forced her to sit down, tied her up, and put a gag in her mouth.

Silence again. The little boy sat down by his mother, crying. I had begun to breathe normally again. We could hear the wheels churning out that monotonous rhythm of a train traveling through the night. We could begin to doze, to rest, to dream. . . .

An hour or two went by like this. Then another scream took our breath away. The woman had broken loose from her bonds and was crying out more loudly than ever:

"Look at the fire! Flames, flames everywhere. . . ."

Once more the young men tied her up and gagged her. They even struck her. People encouraged them:

"Make her be quiet! She's mad! Shut her up! She's not the only one. She can keep her mouth shut. . . ."

They struck her several times on the head—blows that might have killed her. Her little boy clung to her; he did not cry out; he did not say a word. He was not even weeping now.

An endless night. Toward dawn, Madame Schachter calmed down. Crouched in her corner, her bewildered gaze scouring the emptiness, she could no longer see us.

She stayed like that all through the day, dumb, absent, isolated among us. As soon as night fell, she began to scream: "There's a fire over there!" She would point at a spot in space, always the same one. They were tired of hitting her. The heat, the thirst, the pestilential stench, the suffocating lack of air—these were as nothing compared with these screams which tore us to shreds. A few days more and we should all have started to scream too.

But we had reached a station. Those who were next to the windows told us its name:

"Auschwitz."

No one had ever heard that name.

The train did not start up again. The afternoon passed slowly. Then the wagon doors slid open. Two men were allowed to get down to fetch water.

When they came back, they told us that, in exchange for a gold watch, they had discovered that this was the last stop. We would be getting out here. There was a labor camp. Conditions were good. Families would not be split up. Only the young people would go to work in the factories. The old men and invalids would be kept occupied in the fields.

The barometer of confidence soared. Here was a sudden release from the terrors of the previous nights. We gave thanks to God.

Madame Schachter stayed in her corner, wilted, dumb, indifferent to the general confidence. Her little boy stroked her hand.

As dusk fell, darkness gathered inside the wagon. We started to eat our last provisions. At ten in the evening, everyone was looking for a convenient position in which to sleep for a while, and soon we were all asleep. Suddenly:

"The fire! The furnace! Look, over there! . . ."

Waking with a start, we rushed to the window. Yet again we had believed her, even if only for a moment. But there was nothing outside save the darkness of night. With shame in our souls, we went back to our places, gnawed by fear, in spite of ourselves. As she continued to scream, they began to hit her again, and it was with the greatest difficulty that they silenced her.

The man in charge of our wagon called a German officer who was walking about on the platform, and asked him if Madame Schachter could be taken to the hospital car.

"You must be patient," the German replied. "She'll be taken there soon."

Toward eleven o'clock, the train began to move. We pressed against the windows. The convoy was moving slowly. A quarter of an hour later, it slowed down again. Through the windows we could see barbed wire; we realized that this must be the camp.

We had forgotten the existence of Madame Schachter. Suddenly, we heard terrible screams:

"Jews, look! Look through the window! Flames! Look!"

And as the train stopped, we saw this time that flames were gushing out of a tall chimney into the black sky.

Madame Schachter was silent herself. Once more she had become dumb, indifferent, absent, and had gone back to her corner.

We looked at the flames in the darkness. There was an abominable odor floating in the air. Suddenly, our doors opened. Some odd-looking characters, dressed in striped shirts and black trousers leapt into the wagon. They held electric torches and truncheons. They began to strike out to right and left, shouting:

"Everybody get out! Everyone out of the wagon! Quickly!"

We jumped out. I threw a last glance toward Madame Schachter. Her little boy was holding her hand.

In front of us flames. In the air that smell of burning flesh. It must have been about midnight. We had arrived at Birkenau, reception center for Auschwitz.

Three

THE CHERISHED OBJECTS we had brought with us thus far were left behind in the train, and with them, at last, our illusions.

Every two yards or so an SS man held his tommy gun trained on us. Hand in hand we followed the crowd.

An SS noncommissioned officer came to meet us, a truncheon in his hand. He gave the order: "Men to the left! Women to the right!"

Eight words spoken quietly, indifferently, without emotion. Eight short, simple words. Yet that was the moment when I parted from my mother. I had not had time to think, but already I felt the pressure of my father's hand: we were alone. For a part of a second I glimpsed my mother and my sisters moving away to the right. Tzipora held Mother's hand. I saw them disappear into the distance; my mother was stroking my sister's fair hair, as though to protect her, while I walked on with my father and the other men. And I did not know that in that place, at that moment, I was parting from my mother and Tzipora forever. I went on walking. My father held onto my hand.

Behind me, an old man fell to the ground. Near him was an SS man, putting his revolver back in its holster.

My hand shifted on my father's arm. I had one thought—not to lose him. Not to be left alone.

The SS officers gave the order:

"Form fives!"

Commotion. At all costs we must keep together. "Here, kid, how old are you?"

It was one of the prisoners who asked me this. I could not see his face, but his voice was tense and weary.

"I'm not quite fifteen yet."

"No. Eighteen."

"But I'm not," I said. "Fifteen."

"Fool. Listen to what I say."

Then he questioned my father, who replied:

"Fifty."

The other grew more furious than ever.

"No, not fifty. Forty. Do you understand? Eighteen and forty."

He disappeared into the night shadows. A second man came up, spitting oaths at us.

"What have you come here for, you sons of bitches? What are you doing here, eh?"

Someone dared to answer him.

"What do you think? Do you suppose we've come here for our own pleasure? Do you think we asked to come?"

A little more, and the man would have killed him.

"You shut your trap, you filthy swine, or I'll squash you right now! You'd have done better to have hanged yourselves where you were than to come here. Didn't you know what was in store for you at Auschwitz? Haven't you heard about it? In 1944?"

No, we had not heard. No one had told us. He could not believe his ears. His tone of voice became increasingly brutal.

"Do you see that chimney over there? See it? Do you see those flames? (Yes, we did see the flames.) Over there—that's where you're going to be taken. That's your grave, over there. Haven't you realized it yet? You dumb bastards, don't you understand anything? You're going to be burned. Frizzled away. Turned into ashes."

He was growing hysterical in his fury. We stayed motionless, petrified. Surely it was all a nightmare? An unimaginable nightmare?

I heard murmurs around me.

"We've got to do something. We can't let ourselves be killed. We can't go like beasts to the slaughter. We've got to revolt."

There were a few sturdy young fellows among us. They had knives on them, and they tried to incite the others to throw themselves on the armed guards.

One of the young men cried:

"Let the world learn of the existence of Auschwitz. Let everybody hear about it, while they can still escape. . . ."

But the older ones begged their children not to do anything foolish:

"You must never lose faith, even when the sword hangs over your head. That's the teaching of our sages. . . ."

The wind of revolt died down. We continued our march toward the square. In the middle stood the notorious Dr. Mengele (a typical SS officer: a cruel face, but not devoid of intelligence, and wearing a monocle); a conductor's baton in his hand, he was standing among the other officers. The baton moved unremittingly, sometimes to the right, sometimes to the left.

I was already in front of him:

"How old are you?" he asked, in an attempt at a paternal tone of voice.

"Eighteen." My voice was shaking.

"Are you in good health?"

"Yes."

"What's your occupation?"

Should I say that I was a student?

"Farmer," I heard myself say.

This conversation cannot have lasted more than a few seconds. It had seemed like an eternity to me.

The baton moved to the left. I took half a step forward. I wanted to see first where they were sending my father. If he went to the right, I would go after him.

The baton once again pointed to the left for him too. A weight was lifted from my heart.

We did not yet know which was the better side, right or left; which road led to prison and which to the crematory. But for the moment I was happy; I was near my father. Our procession continued to move slowly forward.

Another prisoner came up to us:

"Satisfied ?"

"Yes," someone replied.

"Poor devils, you're going to the crematory."

He seemed to be telling the truth. Not far from us, flames were leaping up from a ditch, gigantic flames. They were burning something. A lorry drew up at the pit and delivered its load—little children. Babies! Yes, I saw it—saw it with my own eyes . . . those children in the flames. (Is it surprising that I could not sleep after that? Sleep had fled from my eyes.)

So this was where we were going. A little farther on was another and larger ditch for adults.

I pinched my face. Was I still alive? Was I awake? I could not believe it. How could it be possible for them to burn people, children, and for the world to keep silent? No, none of this could be true. It was a nightmare. . . . Soon I should wake with a start, my heart pounding, and find myself back in the bedroom of my childhood, among my books. . . .

My father's voice drew me from my thoughts:

"It's a shame . . . a shame that you couldn't have gone with your mother. . . . I saw several boys of your age going with their mothers. . . ."

His voice was terribly sad. I realized that he did not want to see what they were going to do to me. He did not want to see the burning of his only son.

My forehead was bathed in cold sweat. But I told him that I did not believe that they could burn people in our age, that humanity would never tolerate it. . . .

"Humanity? Humanity is not concerned with us. Today anything is allowed. Anything is possible, even these crematories. . . ."

His voice was choking.

"Father," I said, "if that is so, I don't want to wait here. I'm going to run to the electric wire. That would be better than slow agony in the flames."

He did not answer. He was weeping. His body was shaken convulsively. Around us, everyone was weeping. Someone began to recite the Kaddish, the prayer for the dead. I do not know if it has ever happened before, in the long history of the Jews, that people have ever recited the prayer for the dead for themselves.

" *Yitgadal veyitkadach shmé raba.* . . . May His Name be blessed and magnified. . . ." whispered my father.

For the first time, I felt revolt rise up in me. Why should I bless His name? The Eternal, Lord of the Universe, the All-Powerful and Terrible, was silent. What had I to thank Him for?

We continued our march. We were gradually drawing closer to the ditch, from which an infernal heat was rising. Still twenty steps to go. If I wanted to bring about my own death, this was the moment. Our line had now only fifteen paces to cover. I bit my lips so that my father would not hear my teeth chattering. Ten steps still. Eight. Seven. We marched slowly on, as though following a hearse at our own funeral. Four steps more. Three steps. There it was now, right in front of us, the pit and its flames. I gathered all that was left of my strength, so that I could break from the ranks and throw myself upon the barbed wire. In the depths of my heart, I bade farewell to my father, to the whole universe; and, in spite of myself, the words formed themselves and issued in a whisper from my lips: *Yitgadal vey-itkadach shmé raba.* . . . May His name be blessed and magnified. . . . My heart was bursting. The moment had come. I was face to face with the Angel of Death. . . .

No. Two steps from the pit we were ordered to turn to the left and made to go into a barracks.

I pressed my father's hand. He said:

"Do you remember Madame Schachter, in the train?"

Never shall I forget that night, the first night in camp, which has turned my life into one long night, seven times cursed and seven times sealed. Never shall I forget that smoke. Never shall I forget the little faces of the children, whose bodies I saw turned into wreaths of smoke beneath a silent blue sky.

Never shall I forget those flames which consumed my faith forever.

Never shall I forget that nocturnal silence which deprived me, for all eternity, of the desire to live. Never shall I forget those moments which murdered my God and my soul and turned my dreams to dust. Never shall I forget these things, even if I am condemned to live as long as God Himself. Never.

The barracks we had been made to go into was very long. In the roof were some blue-tinged skylights. The antechamber of Hell must look like this. So many crazed men, so many cries, so much bestial brutality!

There were dozens of prisoners to receive us, truncheons in their hands, striking out anywhere, at anyone, without reason. Orders:

"Strip! Fast! *Los!* Keep only your belts and shoes in your hands. . . ."

We had to throw our clothes at one end of the barracks.

There was already a great heap there. New suits and old, torn coats, rags. For us, this was the true equality: nakedness. Shivering with the cold.

Some SS officers moved about in the room, looking for strong men. If they were so keen on strength, perhaps one should try and pass oneself off as sturdy? My father thought the reverse. It was better not to draw attention to oneself. Our fate would then be the same as the others. (Later, we were to learn that he was right. Those who were selected that day were enlisted in the *Sonder-Kommando*, the unit which worked in the crematories. Bela Katz—son of a big tradesman from our town—had arrived at Birkenau with the first transport, a week before us. When he heard of our arrival, he managed to get word to us that, having been chosen for his strength, he had himself put his father's body into the crematory oven.)

Blows continued to rain down.

"To the barber!"

Belt and shoes in hand, I let myself be dragged off to the barbers. They took our hair off with clippers, and shaved off all the hair on our bodies. The same thought buzzed all the time in my head—not to be separated from my father.

Freed from the hands of the barbers, we began to wander in the crowd, meeting friends and acquaintances. These meetings filled us with joy—yes, joy—"Thank God! You're still alive!"

But others were crying. They used all their remaining strength in weeping. Why had they let themselves be brought here? Why couldn't they have died in their beds? Sobs choked their voices.

Suddenly, someone threw his arms round my neck in an embrace: Yechiel, brother of the rabbi of Sighet. He was sobbing bitterly. I thought he was weeping with joy at still being alive.

"Don't cry, Yechiel," I said. "Don't waste your tears. . . ."

"Not cry? We're on the threshold of death. . . . Soon we shall have crossed over. . . . Don't you understand? How could I not cry?"

Through the blue-tinged skylights I could see the darkness gradually fading. I had ceased to feel fear. And then I was overcome by an inhuman weariness.

Those absent no longer touched even the surface of our memories. We still spoke of them—"Who knows what may have become of them?"—but we had little concern for their fate. We were incapable of thinking of anything at all. Our senses were blunted; everything was blurred as in a fog. It was no longer possible to grasp anything. The instincts of self-preservation, of self-defense, of pride, had all deserted us. In one ultimate moment of lucidity it seemed to me that we were damned souls wandering in the half-world, souls condemned to wander through space till the generations of man came to an end, seeking their redemption, seeking oblivion—without hope of finding it.

Toward five o'clock in the morning, we were driven out of the barracks. The Kapos beat us once more, but I had ceased to feel any pain from their blows. An icy wind enveloped us. We were naked, our shoes and belts in our hands. The command: "Run!" And we ran. After a few minutes of racing, a new barracks.

A barrel of petrol at the entrance. Disinfection. Everyone was soaked in it. Then a hot shower. At high speed. As we came out from the water, we were driven outside. More running. Another barracks, the store. Very long tables. Mountains of prison clothes. On we ran. As we passed, trousers, tunic, shirt, and socks were thrown to us.

Within a few seconds, we had ceased to be men. If the situation had not been tragic, we should have roared with laughter. Such outfits! Meir Katz, a giant, had a child's trousers, and Stern, a thin little chap, a tunic which completely swamped him. We immediately began the necessary exchanges.

I glanced at my father. How he had changed! His eyes had grown dim. I would have liked to speak to him, but I did not know what to say.

The night was gone. The morning star was shining in the sky. I too had become a completely different person. The student of the Talmud, the child that I was, had been consumed in the flames. There remained only a shape that looked like me. A dark flame had entered into my soul and devoured it.

So much had happened within such a few hours that I had lost all sense of time. When had we left our houses? And the ghetto? And the train? Was it only a week? One night—*one single night?*

How long had we been standing like this in the icy wind? An hour? Simply an hour? Sixty minutes?

Surely it was a dream.

Not far from us there were some prisoners at work. Some were digging holes, others carrying sand. None of them so much as glanced at us. We were so many dried-up trees in the heart of a desert. Behind me, some people were talking. I had not the slightest desire to listen to what they were saying, to know who was talking or what they were talking about. No one dared to raise his voice, though there was no supervisor near us. People whispered. Perhaps it was because of the thick smoke which poisoned the air and took one by the throat. . . .

We were made to go into a new barracks, in the "gypsies' camp." In ranks of five.

"And now stay where you are!"

There was no floor. A roof and four walls. Our feet sank into the mud.

Another spell of waiting began. I went to sleep standing up. I dreamed of a bed, of my mother's caress. And I woke up: I was standing, my feet in the mud. Some people collapsed and lay where they were. Others cried:

"Are you mad? We've been told to stay standing. Do you want to bring trouble on us all?"

As if all the trouble in the world had not descended already upon our heads! Gradually, we all sat down in the mud. But we had to jump up constantly, every time a Kapo came in to see if anybody had a pair of new shoes. If so, they had to be given up to him. It was no use opposing this: blows rained down and in the final reckoning you had lost your shoes anyway.

I had new shoes myself. But as they were coated with a thick layer of mud, no one had noticed them. I thanked God, in an improvised prayer, for having created mud in His infinite and wonderful universe.

Suddenly the silence grew oppressive. An SS officer had come in and, with him, the odor of the Angel of Death. We stared fixedly at his fleshy lips. From the middle of the barracks, he harangued us:

"You're in a concentration camp. At Auschwitz. . . . "

A pause. He observed the effect his words had produced. His face has stayed in my memory to this day. A tall man, about thirty, with crime inscribed upon his brow and in the pupils of his eyes. He. looked us over as if we were a pack of leprous dogs hanging onto our lives.

"Remember this," he went on. "Remember it forever. Engrave it into your minds. You are at Auschwitz. And Auschwitz is not a convalescent home. It's a concentration camp. Here, you have got to work. If not, you will go straight to the furnace. To the crematory. Work or the crematory— the choice is in your hands."

We had already lived through so much that night, we thought nothing could frighten us any more. But his clipped words made us tremble. Here the word "furnace" was not a word empty of meaning: it floated on the air, mingling with the smoke. It was perhaps the only word which did have any real meaning here. He left the barracks. Kapos appeared, crying:

"All skilled workers—locksmiths, electricians, watchmakers—one step forward!"

The rest of us were made to go to another barracks, a stone one this time. With permission to sit down. A gypsy deportee was in charge of us.

My father was suddenly seized with colic. He got up and went toward the gypsy, asking politely, in German:

"Excuse me, can you tell me where the lavatories are?"

The gypsy looked him up and down slowly, from head to foot. As if he wanted to convince himself that this man addressing him was really a creature of flesh and bone, a living being with a body and a belly. Then, as if he had suddenly woken up from a heavy doze, he dealt my father such a clout that he fell to the ground, crawling back to his place on all fours.

I did not move. What had happened to me? My father had just been struck, before my very eyes, and I had not flickered an eyelid. I had looked on and said nothing. Yesterday, I should have sunk my nails into the criminal's flesh. Had I changed so much, then? So quickly? Now remorse began to gnaw at me. I thought only: I shall never forgive them for that. My father must have guessed my feelings. He whispered in my ear, "It doesn't hurt." His cheek still bore the red mark of the man's hand.

"Everyone outside!"

Ten gypsies had come and joined our supervisor. Whips and truncheons cracked round me. My feet were running without my being aware of it. I tried to hide from the blows behind the others. The spring sunshine.

"Form fives!"

The prisoners whom I had noticed in the morning were working at the side. There was no guard near them, only the shadow of the chimney. . . . Dazed by the sunshine and by my reverie, I felt someone tugging at my sleeve. It was my father. "Come on, my boy."

We marched on. Doors opened and closed again. On we went between the electric wires. At each step, a white placard with a death's head on it stared us in the face. A caption: "Warning. Danger of death." Mockery: was there a single place here where you were not in danger of death?

The gypsies stopped near another barracks. They were replaced by SS, who surrounded us. Revolvers, machine guns, police dogs.

The march had lasted half an hour. Looking around me, I noticed that the barbed wires were behind us. We had left the camp.

It was a beautiful day in May. The fragrance of spring was in the air. The sun was setting in the west.

But we had been marching for only a few moments when we saw the barbed wire of another camp. An iron door with this inscription over it:

"*Work is liberty!*"

Auschwitz.

First impression: this was better than Birkenau. There were two-storied buildings of concrete instead of wooden barracks. There were little gardens here and there. We were led to one of these prison blocks. Seated on the ground by the entrance, we began another session of waiting. Every now and then, someone was made to go in. These were the showers, a compulsory formality at the entrance to all these camps. Even if you were simply passing from one to the other several times a day, you still had to go through the baths every time.

After coming out from the hot water, we stayed shivering in the night air. Our clothes had been left behind in the other block, and we had been promised other outfits.

Toward midnight, we were told to run.

"Faster," shouted our guards. "The faster you run, the sooner you can go to bed."

After a few minutes of this mad race we arrived in front of another block. The prisoner in charge was waiting for us.

He was a young Pole, who smiled at us. He began to talk to us, and, despite our weariness, we listened patiently.

"Comrades, you're in the concentration camp of Auschwitz. There's a long road of suffering ahead of you. But don't lose courage. You've already escaped the gravest danger: selection. So now, muster your strength, and don't lose heart. We shall all see the day of liberation. Have faith in life. Above all else, have faith. Drive out despair, and you will keep death away from yourselves. Hell is not for eternity. And now, a prayer—or rather, a piece of advice: let there be comradeship among you. We are all brothers, and we are all suffering the same fate. The same smoke floats over all our heads. Help one another. It is the only way to survive. Enough said. You're tired. Listen. You're in Block 17. 1 am responsible for keeping order here. Anyone with a complaint against anyone else can come and see me. That's all. You-can go to bed. Two people to a bunk. Good night." The first human words.

No sooner had we climbed into the bunks than we fell into a deep sleep.

The next morning, the "veteran" prisoners treated us without brutality. We went to the wash place. We were given new clothes. We were brought black coffee.

We left the block at about ten o'clock, so that it could be cleaned. Outside the sunshine warmed us. Our morale was much improved. We were feeling the benefit of a night's sleep. Friends met each other, exchanged a few sentences. We talked of everything, except those who had disappeared. The general opinion was that the war was about to end.

At about noon they brought us soup: a plate of thick soup for each person. Tormented though I was by hunger, I refused to touch it. I was still the spoiled child I had always been. My father swallowed my ration.

In the shade of the block, we then had a little siesta. He must have been lying, that SS officer in the muddy barracks. Auschwitz was in fact a rest home. . . .

In the afternoon we were made to line up. Three prisoners brought a table and some medical instruments. With the left sleeve rolled up, each person passed in front of the table. The three "veterans," with needles in their hands, engraved a number on our left arms. I became A-7713. After that I had no other name.

At dusk, roll call. The working units came back. Near the door, the band was playing military marches. Tens of thousands of prisoners stood in rows while the SS checked their numbers.

After roll call, the prisoners from all the blocks scattered to look for friends, relatives, and neighbors who had arrived in the last convoy.

Days passed. In the morning, black coffee. At noon, soup. (By the third day I was eating any kind of soup hungrily.) At six p.m., roll call. Then bread and something. At nine o'clock, bed.

We had already been eight days at Auschwitz. It was during roll call. We were not expecting anything except the sound of the bell which would announce the end of roll call. I suddenly heard someone passing between the rows asking, "Which of you is Wiesel of Sighet?"

The man looking for us was a bespectacled little fellow with a wrinkled, wizened face. My father answered him.

"I'm Wiesel of Sighet."

The little man looked at him for a long while, with his eyes narrowed.

"You don't recognize me—you don't recognize me. I'm a relative of yours. Stein. Have you forgotten me already? Stein! Stein of Antwerp. Reizel's husband. Your wife was Reizel's aunt. She often used to write to us . . . and such letters!"

My father had not recognized him. He must scarcely have known him, since my father was always up to his neck in the affairs of the Jewish community, and much less well versed in family matters. He was always elsewhere, lost in his thoughts. (Once a cousin came to see us at Sighet. She had been staying with us and eating at our table for over a fortnight before my father noticed her presence for the first time.) No, he could not have remembered Stein. As for me, I recognized him at once. I had known his wife Reizel before she left for Belgium.

He said, "I was deported in 1942. 1 heard that a transport had come in from your region, and I came to find you. I thought perhaps you might have news of Reizel and my little boys. They stayed behind in Antwerp. . . ."

I knew nothing about them. Since 1940, my mother had not had a single letter from them. But I lied.

"Yes, my mother's had news from your family. Reizel is very well. The children too. . . ."

He wept with joy. He would have liked to stay longer, to learn more details, to drink in the good news, but an SS came up, and he had to go, calling to us that he would be back the next day.

The bell gave us the signal to disperse. We went to get our evening meal of bread and margarine. I was dreadfully hungry and swallowed my ration on the spot.

My father said, "You don't want to eat it all at once. Tomorrow's another day. . . ."

And seeing that his advice had come too late and that there was nothing left of my ration, he did not even begin his own.

"Personally, I'm not hungry," he said.

We stayed at Auschwitz for three weeks. We had nothing to do. We slept a great deal in the afternoon and at night.

The only worry was to avoid moves, to stay here as long as possible. It was not difficult; it was simply a matter of never putting oneself down as a skilled worker. Laborers were being kept till the end.

At the beginning of the third week, the prisoner in charge of our block was deprived of his office, being considered too humane. Our new head was savage, and his assistants were real monsters. The good days were over.

We began to wonder if it would not be better to let oneself be chosen for the next move.

Stein, our relation from Antwerp, continued to visit us, and from time to time he would bring a half ration of bread.

"Here, this is for you, Eliezer."

Every time he came, there would be tears running down his face, congealing there, freezing. He would often say to my father:

"Take care of your son. He's very weak and dried up. Look after him well, to avoid the selection. Eat! It doesn't matter what or when. Eat everything you can. The weak don't hang about for long here. . . ."

And he was so thin himself, so dried up, so weak. . . .

"The only thing that keeps me alive," he used to say, "is that Reizel and the children are still alive. If it wasn't for them, I couldn't keep going."

He came toward us one evening, his face radiant.

"A transport's just come in from Antwerp. I'm going to see them tomorrow. They'll be sure to have news."

He went off.

We were not to see him again. He had had news. Real news.

In the evening, lying on our beds, we would try to sing some of the Hasidic melodies, and Akiba Drumer would break our hearts with his deep, solemn voice.

Some talked of God, of his mysterious ways, of the sins of the Jewish people, and of their future deliverance. But I had ceased to pray. How I sympathized with Job! I did not deny God's existence, but I doubted His absolute justice.

Akiba Drumer said: "God is testing us. He wants to find out whether we can dominate our base instincts and kill the Satan within us. We have no right to despair. And if he punishes us relentlessly, it's a sign that He loves us all the more."

Hersch Genud, well versed in the cabbala, spoke of the end of the world and the coming of Messiah.

Only occasionally during these conversations did the thought occur to me: "Where is my mother at this moment? And Tzipora . . . ?"

"Your mother is still a young woman," said my father on one occasion. "She must be in a labor camp. And Tzipora's a big girl now, isn't she? She must be in a camp, too."

How we should have liked to believe it. We pretended, for what if the other one should still be believing it?

All the skilled workers had already been sent to other camps. There were only about a hundred of us ordinary laborers left.

"It's your turn today," said the secretary of the block. "You're going with the next transport."

At ten o'clock we were given our daily ration of bread. We were surrounded by about ten SS. On the door the plaque: *"Work is liberty."* We were counted. And then, there we were, right out in the country on the sunny road. In the sky a few little white clouds.

We walked slowly. The guards were in no hurry. We were glad of this. As we went through the villages, many of the Germans stared at us without surprise. They had probably already seen quite a few of these processions.

On the way, we met some young German girls. The guards began to tease them. The girls giggled, pleased. They let themselves be kissed and tickled, exploding with laughter. They were all laughing and joking and shouting blandishments at one another for a good part of the way. During this time, at least we did not have to endure either shouts or blows from the rifle butt.

At the end of four hours, we reached our new camp: Buna. The iron gate closed behind us.

Four

THE CAMP looked as though it had suffered an epidemic: empty and dead. There were just a few well-clad prisoners walking about between the blocks.

Of course, we had to go through the showers first. The head of our camp joined us there. He was a strong, well-built, broad-shouldered man: bull neck, thick lips, frizzled hair. He looked kind. A smile shone from time to time in his gray-blue eyes. Our convoy included a few children ten and twelve years old. The officer took an interest in them and gave orders for them to be brought food.

After we had been given new clothes, we were installed in two tents. We had to wait to be enlisted in the labor units, then we could pass into the block.

That evening, the labor units came back from the work yards. Roll call. We began to look for familiar faces, to seek information, to question the veteran prisoners about which labor unit was the best, which block one should try to get into. The prisoners all agreed, saying, "Buna's a very good camp. You can stand it. The important thing is not to get transferred to the building unit. . . ."

As if the choice were in our own hands.

The head of our tent was a German. An assassin's face, fleshy lips, hands like a wolf's paws. He was so fat he could hardly move. Like the leader of the camp, he loved children. As soon as we arrived, he had brought them bread, soup, and margarine. (Actually, this was not disinterested affection: there was a considerable traffic in children among homosexuals here, I learned later.)

The head told us: "You're staying here three days in quarantine. Then you're going to work. Tomorrow, medical inspection."

One of his assistants—a hard-faced boy, with hooligan's eyes—came up to me:

"Do you want to get into a good unit?"

"I certainly do. But on one condition: I want to stay with my father."

"All right," he said. "I can arrange that. For a small consideration: your shoes. I'll give you some others."

I refused to give him my shoes. They were all I had left.

"I'll give you an extra ration of bread and margarine."

He was very keen on my shoes; but I did not give them up to him. (Later on they were taken from me just the same. But in exchange for nothing this time.)

Medical examination in the open air in the early hours of the morning, before three doctors seated on a bench.

The first barely examined me at all. He was content merely to ask: "Are you in good health?"

Who would have dared say anything to the contrary?

The dentist, on the other hand, seemed most conscientious: he would order us to open our mouths wide. Actually he was not looking for decayed teeth, but gold ones. Anyone who had gold in his mouth had his number added to a list. I myself had a gold crown.

The first three days passed by rapidly. On the fourth day, at dawn, when we were standing in front of the tent, the Kapos appeared. Then each began to choose the men who suited him:

"You . . . you . . . you and you. . . ." They pointed a finger, as though choosing cattle or merchandise.

We followed our Kapo, a young man. He made us stop at the entrance to the first block, near the door of the camp. This was the orchestra block. "Go in," he ordered. We were surprised. What had we to do with music?

The band played a military march, always the same one. Dozens of units left for the workyards, in step. The Kapos beat time: "Left, right, left, right."

Some SS officers, pen and paper in hand, counted the men as they went out. The band went on playing the same march until the last unit had gone by. Then the conductor's baton was still. The band stopped dead, and the Kapos yelled:

"Form fives!"

We left the camp without music, but in step: we still had the sound of the march in our ears.

"Left, right! Left, right!"

We started talking to the musicians next to us.

We drew up in ranks of five, with the musicians. They were nearly all Jews: Juliek, a bespectacled Pole with a cynical smile on his pale face; Louis, a distinguished violinist who came from Holland—he complained that they would not let him play Beethoven: Jews were not allowed to play German music; Hans, a lively young Berliner. The foreman was a Pole, Franek, a former student from Warsaw.

Juliek explained to me: "We work in a warehouse for electrical equipment, not far from here. The work isn't in the least difficult or dangerous. But Idek, the Kapo, has bouts of madness now and then, when it's best to keep out of his way."

"You're lucky, son," smiled Hans. "You've landed in a good unit. . . ."

Ten minutes later, we were in front of the warehouse. A German employee, a civilian, the *meister*, came to meet us. He paid us about as much attention as a dealer might who was just receiving a delivery of old rags.

Our comrades had been right; the work was not difficult. Sitting on the ground, we had to count bolts, bulbs, and small electrical fittings. The Kápo explained to us at great length the vast importance of our work, warning us that anyone found slacking would have him to reckon with. My new comrades reassured me.

"There's nothing to be scared of. He has to say that because of the *meister*."

There were a number of Polish civilians there, and a few French women, who were casting friendly glances at the musicians.

Franek, the foreman, put me in a corner. "Don't kill yourself; there's no hurry. But mind an SS man doesn't catch you unawares."

"Please . . . I would have liked to be by my father."

"All right. Your father'll be working here by your side."

We were lucky.

There were two boys attached to our group: Yossi and Tibi, two brothers. They were Czechs whose parents had been exterminated at Birkenau. They lived, body and soul, for each other.

They and I very soon became friends. Having once belonged to a Zionist youth organization, they knew innumerable Hebrew chants. Thus we would often hum tunes evoking the calm waters of Jordan and the majestic sanctity of Jerusalem. And we would often talk of Palestine. Their parents, like mine, had lacked the courage to wind up their affairs and emigrate while there was still time. We decided that, if we were granted our lives until the liberation, we would not stay in Europe a day longer. We would take the first boat for Haifa.

Still lost in his cabbalistic dreams, Akiba Drumer had discovered a verse in the Bible which, interpreted in terms of numerology, enabled him to predict that the deliverance was due within the coming weeks.

We had left the tents for the musicians' block. We were entitled to a blanket, a wash bowl, and a bar of soap. The head of the block was a German Jew.

It was good to be under a Jew. He was called Alphonse. A young man with an extraordinarily aged face, he was entirely devoted to the cause of "his" block. Whenever he could, he would organize a cauldron of soup for the young ones, the weak, all those who were dreaming more about an extra plateful than of liberty.

One day when we had just come back from the warehouse I was sent for by the secretary of the block.

"A-7713 ?"

"That's me."

"After eating, you're to go to the dentist."

"But I haven't got toothache."

"After eating. Without fail."

I went to the hospital block. There were about twenty prisoners waiting in a queue in front of the door. It did not take long to discover why we had been summoned: it was for the extraction of our gold teeth.

The dentist, a Jew from Czechoslovakia, had a face like a death mask. When he opened his mouth, there was a horrible sight of yellow, decaying teeth. I sat in the chair and asked him humbly: "Please, what are you going to do?"

"Simply take out your gold crown," he replied, indifferently.

I had the idea of pretending to be ill.

"You couldn't wait a few days, Doctor? I don't feel very well. I've got a temperature. . . ."

He wrinkled his brow, thought for a moment, and took my pulse.

"All right, son. When you feel better, come back and see me. But don't wait till I send for you!"

I went to see him a week later. With the same excuse: I still did not feel any better. He did not seem to show any surprise, and I do not know if he believed me. He was probably glad to see that I had come back of my own accord, as I had promised. He gave me another reprieve.

A few days after this visit of mine, they closed the dentist's surgery, and he was thrown into prison. He was going to be hanged. It was alleged that he had been running a private traffic of his own in the prisoners' gold teeth. I did not feel any pity for him. I was even pleased about what had happened. I had saved my gold crown. It might be useful to me one day to buy something—bread or life. I now took little interest in anything except my daily plate of soup and my crust of stale bread. Bread, soup—these were my whole life. I was a body. Perhaps less than that even: a starved stomach. The stomach alone was aware of the passage of time.

At the warehouse I often worked next to a young French girl. We did not speak to one another, since she knew no German and I did not understand French.

She seemed to me to be a Jewess, though here she passed as Aryan. She was a forced labor deportee.

One day when Idek was seized with one of his fits of frenzy, I got in his way. He leapt on me, like a wild animal, hitting me in the chest, on the head, throwing me down and pulling me up again, his blows growing more and more violent, until I was covered with blood. As I was biting my lips to stop myself from screaming with pain, he must have taken my silence for defiance, for he went on hitting me even harder.

Suddenly he calmed down. As if nothing had happened, he sent me back to work. It was as though we had been taking part together in some game where we each had our role to play.

I dragged myself to my corner. I ached all over. I felt a cool hand wiping my blood-stained forehead. It was the French girl. She gave me her mournful smile and slipped a bit of bread into my hand. She looked into my eyes. I felt that she wanted to say something but was choked by fear. For a long moment she stayed like that, then her face cleared and she said to me in almost perfect German:

"Bite your lip, little brother. . . . Don't cry. Keep your anger and hatred for another day, for later on. The day will come, but not now. . . . Wait. Grit your teeth and wait. . . ."

Many years later, in Paris, I was reading my paper in the Metro. Facing me was a very beautiful woman with black hair and dreamy eyes. I had seen those eyes before somewhere. It was she.

"You don't recognize me?"

"I don't know you."

"In 1944 you were in Germany, at Buna, weren't you?"

"Yes. . . ."

"You used to work in the electrical warehouse. . . ."

"Yes," she said, somewhat disturbed. And then, after a moment's silence: "Wait a minute . . . I do remember. . . ."

"Idek, the Kapo . . . the little Jewish boy . . . your kind words. . . ."

We left the Metro together to sit down on the terrace of a cafe. We spent the whole evening reminiscing.

Before I parted from her, I asked her: "May I ask you a question?"

"I know what it will be—go on."

"What?"

"Am I Jewish . . .? Yes, I am Jewish. From a religious family. During the occupation I obtained forged papers and passed myself off as an Aryan. That's how I was enlisted in the forced labor groups, and when I was deported to Germany, I escaped the concentration camp. At the warehouse, no one knew I could speak German. That would have aroused suspicions. Saying those few words to you was risky: but I knew you wouldn't give me away. . . ." Another time we had to load Diesel engines onto trains supervised by German soldiers. Idek's nerves were on edge. He was restraining himself with great difficulty. Suddenly, his frenzy broke out. The victim was my father.

"You lazy old devil!" Idek began to yell. "Do you call that work?"

And he began to beat him with an iron bar. At first my father crouched under the blows, then he broke in two, like a dry tree struck by lightning, and collapsed.

I had watched the whole scene without moving. I kept quiet. In fact I was thinking of how to get farther away so that I would not be hit myself. What is more, any anger I felt at that moment was directed, not against the Kapo, but against my father. I was angry with him, for not knowing how to avoid Idek's outbreak. That is what concentration camp life had made of me.

Franek, the foreman, one day noticed the gold-crowned tooth in my mouth.

"Give me your crown, kid."

I told him it was impossible, that I could not eat without it.

"What do they give you to eat, anyway?"

I found another answer; the crown had been put down on a list after the medical inspection. This could bring trouble on us both.

"If you don't give me your crown, you'll pay for it even more."

This sympathetic, intelligent youth was suddenly no longer the same person. His eyes gleamed with desire. I told him I had to ask my father's advice.

"Ask your father, kid. But I want an answer by tomorrow."

When I spoke to my father about it, he turned pale, was silent a long while, and then said:

"No, son, you mustn't do it."

"He'll take it out on us!"

"He won't dare."

But alas, Franek knew where to touch me; he knew my weak point. My father had never done military service, and he never succeeded in marching in step. Here, every time we moved from one place to another in a body, we marched in strict rhythm. This was Franek's chance to torment my father and to thrash him savagely every day. Left, right: punch! Left, right: clout!

I decided to give my father lessons myself, to teach him to change step, and to keep to the rhythm. We began to do exercises in front of our block. I would give the commands: "Left, right!" and my father would practice. Some of the prisoners began to laugh at us.

"Look at this little officer teaching the old chap to march . . . Hey, general, how many rations of bread does the old boy give you for this?"

But my father's progress was still inadequate, and blows continued to rain down on him.

"So you still can't march in step, you lazy old devil?"

These scenes were repeated for two weeks. We could not stand any more. We had to give in. When the day came, Franek burst into wild laughter.

"I knew it, I knew quite well I would win. Better late than never. And because you've made me wait, that's going to cost you a ration of bread. A ration of bread for one of my pals, a famous dentist from Warsaw, so that he can take your crown out."

"What? My ration of bread so that you can have *my* crown."

Franek grinned.

"What would you like then? Shall I break your teeth with my fist?"

That same evening, in the lavatory the dentist from Warsaw pulled out my crowned tooth, with the aid of a rusty spoon.

Franek grew kinder. Occasionally, he even gave me extra soup. But that did not last long. A fortnight later, all the Poles were transferred to another camp. I had lost my crown for nothing.

A few days before the Poles left, I had a new experience. It was a Sunday morning. Our unit did not need to go to work that day. But all the same Idek would not hear of our staying in the camp. We had to go to the warehouse. This sudden enthusiasm for work left us stunned.

At the warehouse, Idek handed us over to Franek, saying, "Do what you like. But do something. If not, you'll hear from me. . . ."

And he disappeared.

We did not know what to do. Tired of squatting down, we each in turn went for a walk through the warehouse, looking for a bit of bread some civilian might have left behind.

When I came to the back of the building, I heard a noise coming from a little room next door. I went up and saw Idek with a young Polish girl, half-naked, on a mattress. Then I understood why Idek had refused to let us stay in the camp. Moving a hundred prisoners so that he could lie with a girl! It struck me as so funny that I burst out laughing.

Idek leapt up, turned around, and saw me, while the girl tried to cover up her breasts. I wanted to run away, but my legs were glued to the ground. Idek seized me by the throat.

Speaking in a low voice, he said, "You wait and see, kid. . . . You'll soon find out what leaving your work's going to cost you. . . . You're going to pay for this pretty soon. . . . And now, go back to your place."

Half an hour before work usually ended, the Kapo collected together the whole unit. Roll call. Nobody knew what had happened. Roll call at this time of day? Here? But I knew. The Kapo gave a short speech.

"An ordinary prisoner has no right to meddle in other people's affairs. One of you does not seem to have understood this. I'm obliged, therefore, to make it very clear to him once and for all."

I felt the sweat run down my back.

"A-7713 !"

I came forward.

"A box!" he ordered.

They brought him a box.

"Lie down on it! On your stomach!"

I obeyed.

Then I was aware of nothing but the strokes of the whip.

"One . . . two . . .," he counted.

He took his time between each stroke. Only the first ones really hurt me. I could hear him counting:

"Ten . . . eleven . . ."

His voice was calm and reached me as through a thick wall.

"Twenty-three . . ."

Two more, I thought, half conscious. The Kapo waited.

"Twenty-four . . . twenty-five!"

It was over. But I did not realize it, for I had fainted. I felt myself come round as a bucket of cold water was thrown over me. I was still lying on the box. I could just vaguely make out the wet ground surrounding me. Then I heard someone cry out. It must have been the Kapo. I began to distinguish the words he was shouting.

"Get up!"

I probably made some movement to raise myself, because I felt myself falling back onto the box. How I longed to get up!

"Get up!" he yelled more loudly.

If only I could have answered him, at least; if only I could have told him that I could not move! But I could not manage to open my lips.

At Idek's command, two prisoners lifted me up and led me in front of him.

"Look me in the eye!"

I looked at him without seeing him. I was thinking of my father. He must have suffered more than I did.

"Listen to me, you bastard!" said Idek, coldly. "That's for your curiosity. You'll get five times more if you dare tell anyone what you saw! Understand?"

I nodded my head, once, ten times. I nodded ceaselessly. as if my head had decided to say yes without ever stopping.

One Sunday, when half of us—including my father—were at work, the rest—including myself—were in the block, taking advantage of the chance to stay in bed late in the morning.

At about ten o'clock, the air-raid sirens began to wail. An alert. The leaders of the block ran to assemble us inside, while the SS took refuge in the shelters. As it was relatively easy to escape during a warning—the guards left their lookout posts and the electric current was cut off in the barbed-wire fences—the SS had orders to kill anyone found outside the blocks.

Within a few minutes, the camp looked like an abandoned ship. Not a living soul on the paths. Near the kitchen, two cauldrons of steaming hot soup had been left, half full. Two cauldrons of soup, right in the middle of the path, with no one guarding them! A feast for kings, abandoned, supreme temptation! Hundreds of eyes looked at them, sparkling with desire. Two lambs, with a hundred wolves lying in wait for them. Two lambs without a shepherd—a gift. But who would dare?

Terror was stronger than hunger. Suddenly, we saw the door of Block 37 open imperceptibly. A man appeared, crawling like a worm in the direction of the cauldrons.

Hundreds of eyes followed his movements. Hundreds of men crawled with him, scraping their knees with his on the gravel. Every heart trembled, but with envy above all. This man had dared.

He reached the first cauldron. Hearts raced: he had succeeded. jealousy consumed us, burned us up like straw. We never thought for a moment of admiring him. Poor hero, committing suicide for a ration of soup! In our thoughts we were murdering him.

Stretched out by the cauldron, he was now trying to raise himself up to the edge. Either from weakness or fear he stayed there, trying, no doubt, to muster up the last of his strength. At last he succeeded in hoisting himself onto the edge of the pot. For a moment, he seemed to be looking at himself, seeking his ghostlike reflection in the soup. Then, for no apparent reason, he let out a terrible cry, a rattle such as I had never heard before, and, his mouth open, thrust his head toward the still steaming liquid. We jumped at the explosion. Falling back onto the ground, his face stained with soup, the man writhed for a few seconds at the foot of the cauldron, then he moved no more.

Then we began to hear the airplanes. Almost at once, the barracks began to shake.

"They're bombing Buna!" someone shouted.

I thought of my father. But I was glad all the same. To see the whole works go up in fire—what revenge! We had heard so much talk about the defeats of German troops on various fronts, but we did not know how much to believe. This, today, was real!

We were not afraid. And yet, if a bomb had fallen on the blocks, it alone would have claimed hundreds of victims on the spot. But we were no longer afraid of death; at any rate, not of that death. Every bomb that exploded filled us with joy and gave us new confidence in life.

The raid lasted over an hour. If it could only have lasted ten times ten hours! . . . Then silence fell once more. The last sound of an American plane was lost on the wind, and we found ourselves back again in the cemetery. A great trail of black smoke was rising up on the horizon. The sirens began to wail once more. It was the end of the alert.

Everyone came out of the blocks. We filled our lungs with the fire- and smoke-laden air, and our eyes shone with hope. A bomb had fallen in the middle of the camp, near the assembly point, but it had not gone off. We had to take it outside the camp.

The head of the camp, accompanied by his assistant and the chief Kapo, made a tour of inspection along the paths. The raid had left traces of terror on his face.

Right in the middle of the camp lay the body of the man with the soup-stained face, the only victim. The cauldrons were taken back into the kitchen.

The SS had gone back to their lookout posts, behind their machine guns. The interlude was over.

At the end of an hour, we saw the units come back, in step, as usual. Joyfully, I caught sight of my father.

"Several buildings have been flattened right out," he said, "but the warehouse hasn't suffered."

In the afternoon we went cheerfully to clear away the ruins.

A week later, on the way back from work, we noticed in the center of the camp, at the assembly place, a black gallows.

We were told that soup would not be distributed until after roll call. This took longer than usual. The orders were given in a sharper manner than on other days, and in the air there were strange undertones.

"Bare your heads!" yelled the head of the camp, suddenly.

Ten thousand caps were simultaneously removed.

"Cover your heads!"

Ten thousand caps went back onto their skulls, as quick as lightning.

The gate to the camp opened. An SS section appeared and surrounded us: one SS at every three paces. On the lookout towers the machine guns were trained on the assembly place.

"They fear trouble," whispered Juliek.

Two SS men had gone to the cells. They came back with the condemned man between them. He was a youth from Warsaw. He had three years of concentration camp life behind him. He was a strong, well-built boy, a giant in comparison with me.

His back to the gallows, his face turned toward his judge, who was the head of the camp, the boy was pale, but seemed more moved than afraid. His manacled hands did not tremble. His eyes gazed coldly at the hundreds of SS guards, the thousands of prisoners who surrounded him.

The head of the camp began to read his verdict, hammering out each phrase:

"In the name of Himmler . . . prisoner Number . . . stole during the alert. . . . According to the law. . . paragraph prisoner Number . . . is condemned to death. May this be a warning and an example to all prisoners."

No one moved.

I could hear my heart beating. The thousands who had died daily at Auschwitz and at Birkenau in the crematory ovens no longer troubled me. But this one, leaning against his gallows—he overwhelmed me.

"Do you think this ceremony'll be over soon? I'm hungry. . . ." whispered Juliek.

At a sign from the head of the camp, the Lagerkapo advanced toward the condemned man. Two prisoners helped him in his task—for two plates of soup.

The Kapo wanted to bandage the victim's eyes, but he refused.

After a long moment of waiting, the executioner put the rope round his neck. He was on the point of motioning to his assistants to draw the chair away from the prisoner's feet, when the latter cried, in a calm, strong voice:

"Long live liberty! A curse upon Germany! A curse . . .! A cur—"

The executioners had completed their task.

A command cleft the air like a sword.

"Bare your heads."

Ten thousand prisoners paid their last respects.

"Cover your heads!"

Then the whole camp, block after block, had to march past the hanged man and stare at the dimmed eyes, the lolling tongue of death. The Kapos and heads of each block forced everyone to look him full in the face.

After the march, we were given permission to return to the blocks for our meal.

I remember that I found the soup excellent that evening. . . .

I witnessed other hangings. I never saw a single one of the victims weep. For a long time those dried-up bodies had forgotten the bitter taste of tears.

Except once. The Oberkapo of the fifty-second cable unit was a Dutchman, a giant, well over six feet. Seven hundred prisoners worked under his orders, and they all loved him like a brother. No one had ever received a blow at his hands, nor an insult from his lips.

He had a young boy under him, a *pipel*, as they were called—a child with a refined and beautiful face, unheard of in this camp.

(At Buna, the *pipel* were loathed; they were often crueller than adults. I once saw one of thirteen beating his father because the latter had not made his bed properly. The old man was crying softly while the boy shouted: "If you don't stop crying at once I shan't bring you any more bread. Do you understand?" But the Dutchman's little servant was loved by all. He had the face of a sad angel.

One day, the electric power station at Buna was blown up. The Gestapo, summoned to the spot, suspected sabotage. They found a trail. It eventually led to the Dutch Oberkapo. And there, after a search, they found an important stock of arms.

The Oberkapo was arrested immediately. He was tortured for a period of weeks, but in vain. He would not give a single name. He was transferred to Auschwitz. We never heard of him again.

But his little servant had been left behind in the camp in prison. Also put to torture, he too would not speak. Then the SS sentenced him to death, with two other prisoners who had been discovered with arms.

One day when we came back from work, we saw three gallows rearing up in the assembly place, three black crows. Roll call. SS all round us, machine guns trained: the traditional ceremony. Three victims in chains—and one of them, the little servant, the sad-eyed angel.

The SS seemed more preoccupied, more disturbed than usual. To hang a young boy in front of thousands of spectators was no light matter. The head of the camp read the verdict. All eyes were on the child. He was lividly pale, almost calm, biting his lips. The gallows threw its shadow over him.

This time the Lagerkapo refused to act as executioner. Three SS replaced him.

The three victims mounted together onto the chairs.

The three necks were placed at the same moment within the nooses.

"Long live liberty!" cried the two adults.

But the child was silent.

"Where is God? Where is He?" someone behind me asked.

At a sign from the head of the camp, the three chairs tipped over.

Total silence throughout the camp. On the horizon, the sun was setting.

"Bare your heads!" yelled the head of the camp. His voice was raucous. We were weeping.

"Cover your heads!"

Then the march past began. The two adults were no longer alive. Their tongues hung swollen, blue-tinged. But the third rope was still moving; being so light, the child was still alive. . . .

For more than half an hour he stayed there, struggling between life and death, dying in slow agony under our eyes. And we had to look him full in the face. He was still alive when I passed in front of him. His tongue was still red, his eyes were not yet glazed.

Behind me, I heard the same man asking:

"Where is God now?"

And I heard a voice within me answer him:

"Where is He? Here He is—He is hanging here on this gallows. . . ."

That night the soup tasted of corpses.

Five

THE SUMMER WAS coming to an end. The Jewish year was nearly over.

On the eve of Rosh Hashanah, the last day of that accursed year, the whole camp was electric with the tension which was in all our hearts. In spite of everything, this day was different from any other. The last day of the year. The word "last" rang very strangely. What if it were indeed the last day?

They gave us our evening meal, a very thick soup, but no one touched it. We wanted to wait until after prayers. At the place of assembly, surrounded by the electrified barbed wire, thousands of silent Jews gathered, their faces stricken.

Night was falling. Other prisoners continued to crowd in, from every block, able suddenly to conquer time and space and submit both to their will.

"What are You, my God," I thought angrily, "compared to this afflicted crowd, proclaiming to You their faith, their anger, their revolt? What does Your greatness mean, Lord of the Universe, in the face of all this weakness, this decomposition, and this decay? Why do You still trouble their sick minds, their crippled bodies?"

Ten thousand men had come to attend the solemn service, heads of the blocks, Kapos, functionaries of death.

"Bless the Eternal. . . ."

The voice of the officiant had just made itself heard. I thought at first it was the wind.

"Blessed be the Name of the Eternal!"

Thousands of voices repeated the benediction; thousands of men prostrated themselves like trees before a tempest.

"Blessed be the Name of the Eternal!"

Why, but why should I bless Him? In every fiber I rebelled. Because He had had thousands of children burned in His pits? Because He kept six crematories working night and day, on Sundays and feast days? Because in His great might He had created Auschwitz, Birkenau, Buna, and so many factories of death? How could I say to Him: "Blessed art Thou, Eternal, Master of the Universe, Who chose us from among the races to be tortured day and night, to see our fathers, our mothers, our brothers, end in the crematory?

Praised be Thy Holy Name, Thou Who hast chosen us to be butchered on Thine altar?"

I heard the voice of the officiant rising up, powerful yet at the same time broken, amid the tears, the sobs, the sighs of the whole congregation:

"All the earth and the Universe are God's!"

He kept stopping every moment, as though he did not have the strength to find the meaning beneath the words. The melody choked in his throat.

And I, mystic that I had been, I thought:

"Yes, man is very strong, greater than God. When You Were deceived by Adam and Eve, You drove them out of Paradise. When Noah's generation displeased You, You brought down the Flood. When Sodom no longer found favor in Your eyes, You made the sky rain down fire and sulphur. But these men here, whom You have betrayed, whom You have allowed to be tortured, butchered, gassed, burned, what do they do? They pray before You! They praise Your name!"

"All creation bears witness to the Greatness of God!"

Once, New Year's Day had dominated my life. I knew that my sins grieved the Eternal; I implored his forgiveness. Once, I had believed profoundly that upon one solitary deed of mine, one solitary prayer, depended the salvation of the world.

This day I had ceased to plead. I was no longer capable of lamentation. On the contrary, I felt very strong. I was the accuser, God the accused. My eyes were open and I was alone—terribly alone in a world without God and without man. Without love or mercy. I had ceased to be anything but ashes, yet I felt myself to be stronger than the Almighty, to whom my life had been tied for so long. I stood amid that praying congregation, observing it like a stranger.

The service ended with the Kaddish. Everyone recited the Kaddish over his parents, over his children, over his brothers, and over himself.

We stayed for a long time at the assembly place. No one dared to drag himself away from this mirage. Then it was time to go to bed and slowly the prisoners made their way over to their blocks. I heard people wishing one another a Happy New Year!

I ran off to look for my father. And at the same time I was afraid of having to wish him a Happy New Year when I no longer believed in it.

He was standing near the wall, bowed down, his shoulders sagging as though beneath a heavy burden. I went up to him, took his hand and kissed it. A tear fell upon it. Whose was that tear? Mine? His? I said nothing. Nor did he. We had never understood one another so clearly.

The sound of the bell jolted us back to reality. We must go to bed. We came back from far away. I raised my eyes to look at my father's face leaning over mine, to try to discover a smile or something resembling one upon the aged, dried-up countenance. Nothing. Not the shadow of an expression. Beaten.

Yom Kippur. The Day of Atonement.

Should we fast? The question was hotly debated. To fast would mean a surer, swifter death. We fasted here the whole year round. The whole year was Yom Kippur. But others said that we should fast simply because it was dangerous to do so. We should show God that even here, in this enclosed hell, we were capable of singing His praises.

I did not fast, mainly to please my father, who had forbidden me to do so. But further, there was no longer any reason why I should fast. I no longer accepted God's silence. As I swallowed my bowl of soup, I saw in the gesture an act of rebellion and protest against Him.

And I nibbled my crust of bread.

In the depths of my heart, I felt a great void.

The SS gave us a fine New Year's gift.

We had just come back from work. As soon as we had passed through the door of the camp, we sensed something different in the air. Roll call did not take so long as usual. The evening soup was given out with great speed and swallowed down at once in anguish.

I was no longer in the same block as my father. I had been transferred to another unit, the building one, where, twelve hours a day, I had to drag heavy blocks of stone about. The head of my new block was a German Jew, small of stature, with piercing eyes. He told us that evening that no one would be allowed to go out after the evening soup. And soon a terrible word was circulating—selection.

We knew what that meant. An SS man would examine us. Whenever he found a weak one, a *musulman* as we called them, he would write his number down: good for the crematory.

After soup, we gathered together between the beds. The veterans said:

"You're lucky to have been brought here so late. This camp is paradise today, compared with what it was like two years ago. Buna was a real hell then. There was no water, no blankets, less soup and bread. At night we slept almost naked, and it was below thirty degrees. The corpses were collected in hundreds every day. The work was hard. Today, this is a little paradise. The Kapos had orders to kill a certain number of prisoners every day. And every week—selection. A merciless selection. . . . Yes, you're lucky."

"Stop it! Be quiet!" I begged. "You can tell your stories tomorrow or on some other day."

They burst out laughing. They were not veterans for nothing.

"Are you scared? So were we scared. And there was plenty to be scared of in those days."

The old men stayed in their corner, dumb, motionless, hunted. Some were praying.

An hour's delay. In an hour, we should know the verdict—death or a reprieve.

And my father? Suddenly I remembered him. How would he pass the selection? He had aged so much. . . .

The head of our block had never been outside concentration camps since 1933. He had already been through all the slaughterhouses, all the factories of death. At about nine o'clock, he took up his position in our midst:

"Achtung!"

There was instant silence.

"Listen carefully to what I am going to say." (For the first time, I heard his voice quiver.) "In a few moments the selection will begin. You must get completely undressed. Then one by one you go before the SS doctors. I hope you will all succeed in getting through. But you must help your own chances. Before you go into the next room, move about in some way so that you give yourselves a little color. Don't walk slowly, run! Run as if the devil were after you! Don't look at the SS. Run, straight in front of you!"

He broke off for a moment, then added:

"And, the essential thing, don't be afraid!"

Here was a piece of advice we should have liked very much to be able to follow.

I got undressed, leaving my clothes on the bed. There was no danger of anyone stealing them this evening.

Tibi and Yossi, who had changed their unit at the same time as I had, came up to me and said:

"Let's keep together. We shall be stronger."

Yossi was murmuring something between his teeth. He must have been praying. I had never realized that Yossi was a believer. I had even always thought the reverse. Tibi was silent, very pale. All the prisoners in the block stood naked between the beds. This must be how one stands at the last judgment.

"They're coming!"

There were three SS officers standing round the notorious Dr. Mengele, who had received us at Birkenau. The head of the block, with an attempt at a smile, asked us:

"Ready?"

Yes, we were ready. So were the SS doctors. Dr. Mengele was holding a list in his hand: our numbers. He made a sign to the head of the block: "We can begin!" As if this were a game!

The first to go by were the "officials" of the block: *Stubenaelteste*, Kapos, foremen, all in perfect physical condition of course! Then came the ordinary prisoners' turn. Dr. Mengele took stock of them from head to foot. Every now and then, he wrote a number down. One single thought filled my mind: not to let my number be taken; not to show my left arm.

There were only Tibi and Yossi in front of me. They passed. I had time to notice that Mengele had not written their numbers down. Someone pushed me. It was my turn. I ran without looking back. My head was spinning: you're too thin, you're weak, you're too thin, you're good for the furnace. . . . The race seemed interminable. I thought I had been running for years. . . . You're too thin, you're too weak. . . . At last I had arrived exhausted. When I regained my breath, I questioned Yossi and Tibi:

"Was I written down?"

"No," said Yossi. He added, smiling: "In any case, he couldn't have written you down, you were running too fast. . . ."

I began to laugh. I was glad. I would have liked to kiss him. At that moment, what did the others matter! I hadn't been written down.

Those whose numbers had been noted stood apart, abandoned by the whole world. Some were weeping in silence.

The SS officers went away. The head of the block appeared, his face reflecting the general weariness.

"Everything went off all right. Don't worry. Nothing is going to happen to anyone. To anyone."

Again he tried to smile. A poor, emaciated, dried-up Jew questioned him avidly in a trembling voice:

"But . . . but, *Blockaelteste*, they did write me down!"

The head of the block let his anger break out. What! Did someone refuse to believe him!

"What's the matter now? Am I telling lies then? I tell you once and for all, nothing's going to happen to you! To anyone! You're wallowing in your own despair, you fool!"

The bell rang, a signal that the selection had been completed throughout the camp.

With all my might I began to run to Block 36. 1 met my father on the way. He came up to me:

"Well? So you passed?"

"Yes. And you?"

"Me too."

How we breathed again, now! My father had brought me a present— half a ration of bread obtained in exchange for a piece of rubber, found at the warehouse, which would do to sole a shoe.

The bell. Already we must separate, go to bed. Everything was regulated by the bell. It gave me orders, and I automatically obeyed them. I hated it. Whenever I dreamed of a better world, I could only imagine a universe with no bells.

Several days had elapsed. We no longer thought about the selection. We went to work as usual, loading heavy stones into railway wagons. Rations had become more meager: this was the only change.

We had risen before dawn, as on every day. We had received the black coffee, the ration of bread. We were about to set out for the yard as usual. The head of the block arrived, running.

"Silence for a moment. I have a list of numbers here. I'm going to read them to you. Those whose numbers I call won't be going to work this morning; they'll stay behind in the camp."

And, in a soft voice, he read out about ten numbers. We had understood. These were numbers chosen at the selection. Dr. Mengele had not forgotten.

The head of the block went toward his room. Ten prisoners surrounded him, hanging onto his clothes:

"Save us! You promised . . .! We want to go to the yard. We're strong enough to work. We're good workers. We can . . . we will. . . ."

He tried to calm them, to reassure them about their fate, to explain to them that the fact that they were staying behind in the camp did not mean much, had no tragic significance.

"After all, I stay here myself every day," he added.

It was a somewhat feeble argument. He realized it, and without another word went and shut himself up in his room.

The bell had just rung.

"Form up!"

It scarcely mattered now that the work was hard. The essential thing was to be as far away as possible from the block, from the crucible of death, from the center of hell.

I saw my father running toward me. I became frightened all of a sudden.

"What's the matter?"

Out of breath, he could hardly open his mouth.

"Me, too . . . me, too . . .! They told me to stay behind in the camp."

They had written down his number without his being aware of it.

"What will happen?" I asked in anguish.

But it was he who tried to reassure me.

"It isn't certain yet. There's still a chance of escape. They're going to do another selection today . . . a decisive selection."

I was silent.

He felt that his time was short. He spoke quickly. He would have liked to say so many things. His speech grew confused; his voice choked. He knew that I would have to go in a few moments. He would have to stay behind alone, so very alone.

"Look, take this knife," he said to me. "I don't need it any longer. It might be useful to you. And take this spoon as well. Don't sell them. Quickly! Go on. Take what I'm giving you!"

The inheritance.

"Don't talk like that, father." (I felt that I would break into sobs.) "I don't want you to say that. Keep the spoon and knife. You need them as much as I do. We shall see each other again this evening, after work."

He looked at me with his tired eyes, veiled with despair. He went on:

"I'm asking this of you. . . . Take them. Do as I ask, my son. We have no time. . . . Do as your father asks."

Our Kapo yelled that we should start.

The unit set out toward the camp gate. Left, right! I bit my lips. My father had stayed by the block, leaning against the wall. Then he began to run, to catch up with us. Perhaps he had forgotten something he wanted to say to me. . . . But we were marching too quickly. . . . Left, right!

We were already at the gate. They counted us, to the din of military music. We were outside.

The whole day, I wandered about as if sleepwalking. Now and then Tibi and Yossi would throw me a brotherly word. The Kapo, too, tried to reassure me. He had given me easier work today. I felt sick at heart. How well they were treating me! Like an orphan! I thought: even now, my father is still helping me.

I did not know myself what I wanted—for the day to pass quickly or not. I was afraid of finding myself alone that night. How good it would be to die here!

At last we began the return journey. How I longed for orders to run!

The military march. The gate. The camp.

I ran to Block 36.

Were there still miracles on this earth? He was alive. He had escaped the second selection. He had been able to prove that he was still useful. . . . I gave him back his knife and spoon.

Akiba Drumer left us, a victim of the selection. Lately, he had wandered among us, his eyes glazed, telling everyone of his weakness: "I can't go on . . . It's all over. . . ." It was impossible to raise his morale. He didn't listen to what we told him. He could only repeat that all was over for him, that he could no longer keep up the struggle, that he had no strength left, nor faith. Suddenly his eyes would become blank, nothing but two open wounds, two pits of terror.

He was not the only one to lose his faith during those selection days. I knew a rabbi from a little town in Poland, a bent old man, whose lips were always trembling. He used to pray all the time, in the block, in the yard, in the ranks. He would recite whole pages of the Talmud from memory, argue with himself, ask himself questions and answer himself. And one day he said to me: "It's the end. God is no longer with us."

And, as though he had repented of having spoken such words, so clipped, so cold, he added in his faint voice:

"I know. One has no right to say things like that. I know. Man is too small, too humble and inconsiderable to seek to understand the mysterious ways of God. But what can I do? I'm not a sage, one of the elect, nor a saint. I'm just an ordinary creature of flesh and blood. I've got eyes, too, and I can see what they're doing here. Where is the divine Mercy? Where is God? How can I believe, how could anyone believe, in this merciful God?"

Poor Akiba Drumer, if he could have gone on believing in God, if he could have seen a proof of God in this Calvary, he would not have been taken by the selection. But as soon as he felt the first cracks forming in his faith, he had lost his reason for struggling and had begun to die.

When the selection came, he was condemned in advance, offering his own neck to the executioner. All he asked of us was:

"In three days I shall no longer be here. . . . Say the Kaddish for me."

We promised him. In three days' time, when we saw the smoke rising from the chimney, we would think of him. Ten of us would gather together and hold a special service. All his friends would say the Kaddish.

Then he went off toward the hospital, his step steadier, not looking back. An ambulance was waiting to take him to Birkenau.

These were terrible days. We received more blows than food; we were crushed with work. And three days after he had gone we forgot to say the Kaddish.

Winter had come. The days were short, and the nights had become almost unbearable. In the first hours of dawn, the icy wind cut us like a whip. We were given winter clothes —slightly thicker striped shirts. The veterans found in this a new source of derision.

"Now you'll really be getting a taste of the camp!"

We left for work as usual, our bodies frozen. The stones were so cold that it seemed as though our hands would be glued to them if we touched them. But you get used to anything.

On Christmas and New Year's Day, there was no work.

We were allowed a slightly thicker soup.

Toward the middle of January, my right foot began to swell because of the cold. I was unable to put it on the ground. I went to have it examined. The doctor, a great Jewish doctor, a prisoner like ourselves, was quite definite: I must have an operation! If we waited, the toes—and perhaps the whole leg—would have to be amputated.

This was the last straw! But I had no choice. The doctor had decided on an operation, and there was no discussing it. I was even glad that it was he who had made the decision.

They put me into a bed with white sheets. I had forgotten that people slept in sheets.

The hospital was not bad at all. We were given good bread and thicker soup. No more bell. No more roll call. No more work. Now and then I was able to send a bit of bread to my father.

Near me lay a Hungarian Jew who had been struck down with dysentery—skin and bone, with dead eyes. I could only hear his voice; it was the sole indication that he was alive. Where did he get the strength to talk?

"You mustn't rejoice too soon, my boy. There's selection here too. More often than outside. Germany doesn't need sick Jews. Germany doesn't need me. When the next transport comes, you'll have a new neighbor. So listen to me, and take my advice: get out of the hospital before the next selection!"

These words which came from under the ground, from a faceless shape, filled me with terror. It was indeed true that the hospital was very small and that if new invalids arrived in the next few days, room would have to be found for them.

But perhaps my faceless neighbor, fearing that he would be among the first victims, simply wanted to drive me away, to free my bed in order to give himself a chance to survive. Perhaps he just wanted to frighten me. Yet, what if he were telling the truth? I decided to await events.

The doctor came to tell me that the operation would be the next day.

"Don't be afraid," he added. "Everything will be all right."

At ten o'clock in the morning, they took me into the operating room. "My" doctor was there. I took comfort from this. I felt that nothing serious could happen while he was there. There was balm in every word he spoke, and every glance he gave me held a message of hope.

"It will hurt you a bit," he said, "but that will pass. Grit your teeth."

The operation lasted an hour. They had not put me to sleep. I kept my eyes fixed upon my doctor. Then I felt myself go under. . . .

When I came round, opening my eyes, I could see nothing at first but a great whiteness, my sheets; then I noticed the face of my doctor, bending over me:

"Everything went off well. You're brave, my boy. Now you're going to stay here for two weeks, rest comfortably, and it will be over. You'll eat well, and relax your body and your nerves."

I could only follow the movements of his lips. I scarcely understood what he was saying, but the murmur of his voice did me good. Suddenly a cold sweat broke out on my forehead. I could not feel my leg! Had they amputated it?

"Doctor," I stammered. "Doctor. . . ."

"What's the matter, son?"

I lacked the courage to ask him the question.

"Doctor, I'm thirsty. . . ."

He had water brought to me. He was smiling. He was getting ready to go and visit the other patients.

"Doctor?"

"What?"

"Shall I still be able to use my leg?"

He was no longer smiling. I was very frightened. He said:

"Do you trust me, my boy?"

"I trust you absolutely, Doctor."

"Well then, listen to me. You'll be completely recovered in a fortnight. You'll be able to walk like anyone else. The sole of your foot was all full of pus. We just had to open the swelling. You haven't had your leg amputated. You'll see. In a fortnight's time you'll be walking about like everyone else."

I had only a fortnight to wait.

Two days after my operation, there was a rumor going round the camp that the front had suddenly drawn nearer. The Red Army, they said, was advancing on Buna; it was only a matter of hours now.

We were already accustomed to rumors of this kind. It was not the first time a false prophet had foretold to us peace-on-earth, negotiations-with-the-Red-Cross-for-our release, or other false rumors. . . . And often we believed them. It was an injection of morphine.

But this time these prophecies seemed more solid. During these last few nights, we had heard the guns in the distance.

My neighbor, the faceless one, said:

"Don't let yourself be fooled with illusions. Hitler has made it very clear that he will annihilate all the Jews before the clock strikes twelve, before they can hear the last stroke."

I burst out:

"What does it matter to you? Do we have to regard Hitler as a prophet?"

His glazed, faded eyes looked at me. At last he said in a weary voice:

"I've got more faith in Hitler than in anyone else. He's the only one who's kept his promises, all his promises, to the Jewish people."

At four o'clock on the afternoon of the same day, as usual the bell summoned all the heads of the blocks to go and report.

They came back shattered. They could only just open their lips enough to say the word: evacuation. The camp was to be emptied, and we were to be sent farther back. Where to? To somewhere right in the depths of Germany, to other camps; there was no shortage of them.

"When?"

"Tomorrow evening."

"Perhaps the Russians will arrive first."

"Perhaps."

We knew perfectly well that they would not.

The camp had become a hive. People ran about, shouting at one another. In all the blocks, preparations for the journey were going on. I had forgotten about my bad foot. A doctor came into the room and announced:

"Tomorrow, immediately after nightfall, the camp will set out. Block after block. Patients will stay in the infirmary. They will not be evacuated."

This news made us think. Were the SS going to leave hundreds of prisoners to strut about in the hospital blocks, waiting for their liberators? Were they going to let the Jews hear the twelfth stroke sound? Obviously not.

"All the invalids will be summarily killed," said the faceless one. "And sent to the crematory in a final batch."

"The camp is certain to be mined," said another. "The moment the evacuation's over, it'll blow up."

As for me, I was not thinking about death, but I did not want to be separated from my father. We had already suffered so much, borne so much together; this was not the time to be separated.

I ran outside to look for him. The snow was thick, and the windows of the blocks were veiled with frost. One shoe in my hand, because it would not go onto my right foot, I ran on, feeling neither pain nor cold.

"What shall we do?"

My father did not answer.

"What shall we do, father?"

He was lost in thought. The choice was in our hands. For once we could decide our fate for ourselves. We could both stay in the hospital, where I could, thanks to my doctor, get him entered as a patient or a nurse. Or else we could follow the others.

"Well, what shall we do, father?"

He was silent.

"Let's be evacuated with the others," I said to him.

He did not answer. He looked at my foot.

"Do you think you can walk?"

"Yes, I think so."

"Let's hope that we shan't regret it, Eliezer."

I learned after the war the fate of those who had stayed behind in the hospital. They were quite simply liberated by the Russians two days after the evacuation.

I did not go back to the hospital again. I returned to my block. My wound was open and bleeding; the snow had grown red where I had trodden.

The head of the block gave out double rations of bread and margarine, for the journey. We could take as many shirts and other clothes as we liked from the store.

It was cold. We got into bed.

The last night in Buna. Yet another last night. The last night at home, the last night in the ghetto, the last night in the train, and, now, the last night in Buna. How much longer were our lives to be dragged out from one "last night" to another?

I did not sleep at all. Through the frosted panes bursts of red light could be seen. Cannon shots split the nighttime silence. How close the Russians were! Between them and us—one night, our last night. There was whispering from one bed to another: with luck the Russians would be here before the evacuation. Hope revived again.

Someone shouted:

"Try and sleep. Gather your strength for the journey."

This reminded me of my mother's last words of advice in the ghetto.

But I could not sleep. My foot felt as if it were burning.

In the morning, the face of the camp had changed. Prisoners appeared in strange outfits: it was like a masquerade. Everyone had put on several garments, one on top of the other, in order to keep out the cold. Poor mountebanks, wider than they were tall, more dead than alive; poor clowns, their ghostlike faces emerging from piles of prison clothes! Buffoons!

I tried to find a shoe that was too large. In vain. I tore up a blanket and wrapped my wounded foot in it. Then I went wandering through the camp, looking for a little more bread and a few potatoes.

Some said we were being taken to Czechoslovakia. No, to Gros-Rosen. No, to Gleiwitz. No, to. . . .

Two o'clock in the afternoon. The snow was still coming down thickly.

The time was passing quickly now. Dusk had fallen. The day was disappearing in a monochrome of gray.

The head of the block suddenly remembered that he had forgotten to

clean out the block. He ordered four prisoners to wash the wooden floor. . . .
An hour before leaving the camp! Why? For whom?

"For the liberating army," he cried. "So that they'll realize there were
men living here and not pigs."

Were we men then? The block was cleaned from top to bottom, washed
in every corner.

At six o'clock the bell rang. The death knell. The burial. The procession
was about to begin its march.

"Form up! Quickly!"

In a few moments we were all in rows, by blocks. Night had fallen.
Everything was in order, according to the prearranged plan.

The searchlights came on. Hundreds of armed SS men rose up out of the
darkness, accompanied by sheepdogs. The snow never ceased.

The gates of the camp opened. It seemed that an even darker night was
waiting for us on the other side.

The first blocks began to march. We waited. We had to wait for the departure of the fifty-six blocks who came before us. It was very cold. In my
pocket I had two pieces of bread. With how much pleasure could I have
eaten them! But I was not allowed to. Not yet.

Our turn was coming: Block 53 . . . Block 55 . . .

Block 57, forward march!

It snowed relentlessly.

Six

AN ICY WIND blew in violent gusts. But we marched without faltering.

The SS made us increase our pace. "Faster, you swine, you filthy sons of bitches!" Why not? The movement warmed us up a little. The blood flowed more easily in our veins. One felt oneself reviving. . . .

"Faster, you filthy sons of bitches!" We were no longer marching; we were running. Like automatons. The SS were running too, their weapons in their hands. We looked as though we were fleeing before them.

Pitch darkness. Every now and then, an explosion in the night. They had orders to fire on any who could not keep up. Their fingers on the triggers, they did not deprive themselves of this pleasure. If one of us stopped for a second, a sharp shot finished off another filthy son of a bitch.

I was putting one foot in front of the other mechanically. I was dragging with me this skeletal body which weighed so much. If only I could have got rid of it! In spite of my efforts not to think about it, I could feel myself as two entities—my body and me. I hated it.

I repeated to myself: "Don't think. Don't stop. Run."

Near me, men were collapsing in the dirty snow. Shots.

At my side marched a young Polish lad called Zalman. He had been working in the electrical warehouse at Buna. They had laughed at him because he was always praying or meditating on some problem of the Talmud. It was his way of escaping from reality, of not feeling the blows. . . .

He was suddenly seized with cramp in the stomach. "I've got stomach ache," he whispered to me. He could not go on. He had to stop for a moment. I begged him:

"Wait a bit, Zalman. We shall all be stopping soon. We're not going to run like this till the end of the world."

But as he ran he began to undo his buttons, crying:

"I can't go on any longer. My stomach's bursting. . . ."

"Make an effort, Zalman. . . . Try . . ."

"I can't. . . ." he groaned.

His trousers lowered, he let himself sink down.

That is the last picture I have of him. I do not think it can have been the SS who finished him, because no one had noticed. He must have been trampled to death beneath the feet of the thousands of men who followed us.

I quickly forgot him. I began to think of myself again. Because of my painful foot, a shudder went through me at each step. "A few more yards," I thought. "A few more yards, and that will be the end. I shall fall. A spurt of red flame. A shot." Death wrapped itself around me till I was stifled. It stuck to me. I felt that I could touch it. The idea of dying, of no longer being, began to fascinate me. Not to exist any longer. Not to feel the horrible pains in my foot. Not to feel anything, neither weariness, nor cold, nor anything. To break the ranks, to let oneself slide to the edge of the road. . . .

My father's presence was the only thing that stopped me. . . . He was running at my side, out of breath, at the end of his strength, at his wit's end. I had no right to let myself die. What would he do without me? I was his only support.

These thoughts had taken up a brief space of time, during which I had gone on running without feeling my throbbing foot, without realizing that I was running, without being conscious that I owned a body galloping there on the road in the midst of so many thousands of others.

When I came to myself again, I tried to slacken the pace. But there was no way. A great tidal wave of men came rolling onward and would have crushed me like an ant.

I was simply walking in my sleep. I managed to close my eyes and to run like that while asleep. Now and then, someone would push me violently from behind, and I would wake up. The other would shout: "Run faster. If you don't want to go on, let other people come past." All I had to do was to close my eyes for a second to see a whole world passing by, to dream a whole lifetime.

An endless road. Letting oneself be pushed by the mob; letting oneself be dragged along by a blind destiny. When the SS became tired, they were changed. But no one changed us. Our limbs numb with cold despite the running, our throats parched, famished, breathless, on we went.

We were masters of nature, masters of the world. We had forgotten everything—death, fatigue, our natural needs. Stronger than cold or hunger, stronger than the shots and the desire to die, condemned and wandering, mere numbers, we were the only men on earth.

At last, the morning star appeared in the gray sky. A trail of indeterminate light showed on the horizon. We were exhausted. We were without strength, without illusions.

The commandant announced that we had already covered forty-two miles since we left. It was a long time since we had passed beyond the limits of fatigue. Our legs were moving mechanically, in spite of us, without us.

We went through a deserted village. Not a living soul. Not the bark of a dog. Houses with gaping windows. A few slipped out of the ranks to try and hide in some deserted building.

Still one hour's marching more, and at last came the order to rest.

We sank down as one man in the snow. My father shook me.

"Not here. . . . Get up. . . . A little farther on. There's a shed over there . . . come on."

I had neither the will nor the strength to get up. Nevertheless I obeyed. It was not a shed, but a brick factory with a caved-in roof, broken windows, walls filthy with soot. It was not easy to get in. Hundreds of prisoners were crowding at the door.

We at last succeeded in getting inside. There too the snow was thick. I let myself sink down. It was only then that I really felt my weariness. The snow was like a carpet, very gentle, very warm. I fell asleep.

I do not know how long I slept. A few moments or an hour. When I woke up, a frozen hand was patting my cheeks. I forced myself to open my eyes. It was my father.

How old he had grown since the night before! His body was completely twisted, shriveled up into itself. His eyes were petrified, his lips withered, decayed. Everything about him bore witness to extreme exhaustion. His voice was damp with tears and snow:

"Don't let yourself be overcome by sleep, Eliezer. It's dangerous to fall asleep in the snow. You might sleep for good. Come on, come on. Get up."

Get up? How could I? How could I get myself out of this fluffy bed? I could hear what my father said, but it seemed empty of meaning, as though he had told me to lift up the whole building in my arms. . . .

"Come on, son, come on. . . ."

I got up, gritting my teeth. Supporting me with his arm, he led me outside. It was far from easy. It was as difficult to go out as to get in. Under our feet were men crushed, trampled underfoot, dying. No one paid any attention.

We were outside. The icy wind stung my face. I bit my lips continually to prevent them from freezing. Around me everything was dancing a dance of death. It made my head reel. I was walking in a cemetery, among stiffened corpses, logs of wood., Not a cry of distress, not a groan, nothing but a mass agony, in silence. No one asked anyone else for help. You died because you had to die. There was no fuss.

In every stiffened corpse I saw myself. And soon I should not even see them; I should be one of them—a matter of hours.

"Come on, father , let's go back to the shed. . . ."

He did not answer. He was not looking at the dead.

"Come on, father, it's better over there. We can lie down a bit, one after the other. I'll watch over you, and then you can watch over me. We won't let each other fall asleep. We'll look after each other."

He agreed. Trampling over living bodies and corpses, we managed to re-enter the shed. Here we let ourselves sink down.

"Don't be afraid, son. Sleep—you can sleep. I'll look after you myself."

"No, you first, father. Go to sleep."

He refused. I lay down and tried to force myself to sleep, to doze a little, but in vain. God knows what I would not have given for a few moments of sleep. But, deep down, I felt that to sleep would mean to die. And something within me revolted against this death. All round me death was moving in, silently, without violence. It would seize upon some sleeping being, enter into him, and consume him bit by bit. Next to me there was someone trying to wake up his neighbor, his brother, perhaps, or a friend. In vain. Discouraged in the attempt, the man lay down in his turn, next to the corpse, and slept too. Who was there to wake him up? Stretching out an arm, I touched him:

"Wake up. You mustn't sleep here. . . ."

He half opened his eyes.

"No advice," he said in a faint voice. "I'm tired. Leave me alone. Leave me."

My father, too, was gently dozing. I could not see his eyes. His cap had fallen over his face.

"Wake up," I whispered in his ear.

He started up. He sat up and looked round him, bewildered, stupefied—a bereaved stare. He stared all round him in a circle as though he had suddenly decided to draw up an inventory of his universe, to find out exactly where he was, in what place, and why. Then he smiled.

I shall always remember that smile. From which world did it come?

The snow continued to fall in thick flakes over the corpses.

The door of the shed opened. An old man appeared, his moustache covered with frost, his lips blue with cold. It was Rabbi Eliahou, the rabbi of a small Polish community. He was a very good man, well loved by everyone in the camp, even by the Kapos and the heads of the blocks. Despite the trials and privations, his face still shone with his inner purity. He was the only rabbi who was always addressed as "Rabbi" at Buna. He was like one of the old prophets, always in the midst of his people to comfort them. And, strangely, his words of comfort never provoked rebellion; they really brought peace.

He came into the shed and his eyes, brighter than ever, seemed to be looking for someone:

"Perhaps someone has seen my son somewhere?"

He had lost his son in the crowd. He had looked in vain among the dying. Then he had scratched up the snow to find his corpse. Without result.

For three years they had stuck together. Always near each other, for suffering, for blows, for the ration of bread, for prayer. Three years, from camp to camp, from selection to selection. And now—when the end seemed near—fate had separated them. Finding himself near me, Rabbi Eliahou whispered:

"It happened on the road. We lost sight of one another during the journey. I had stayed a little to the rear of the column. I hadn't any strength left for running. And my son didn't notice. That's all I know. Where has he disappeared? Where can I find him? Perhaps you've seen him somewhere?"

"No, Rabbi Eliahou, I haven't seen him."

He left then as he had come: like a wind-swept shadow.

He had already passed through the door when I suddenly remembered seeing his son running by my side. I had forgotten that, and I didn't tell Rabbi Eliahou!

Then I remembered something else: his son had seen him losing ground, limping, staggering back to the rear of the column. He had seen him. And he had continued to run on in front, letting the distance between them grow greater.

A terrible thought loomed up in my mind: he had wanted to get rid of his father! He had felt that his father was growing weak, he had believed that the end was near and had sought this separation in order to get rid of the burden, to free himself from an encumbrance which could lessen his own chances of survival.

I had done well to forget that. And I was glad that Rabbi Eliahou should continue to look for his beloved son.

And, in spite of myself, a prayer rose in my heart, to that God in whom I no longer believed.

My God, Lord of the Universe, give me strength never to do what Rabbi Eliahou's son has done.

Shouts rose outside in the yard, where darkness had fallen. The SS ordered the ranks to form up.

The march began again. The dead stayed in the yard under the snow, like faithful guards assassinated, without burial. No one had said the prayer for the dead over them. Sons abandoned their fathers' remains without a tear.

On the way it snowed, snowed, snowed endlessly. We were marching more slowly. The guards themselves seemed tired. My wounded foot no longer hurt me. It must have been completely frozen. The foot was lost to me. It had detached itself from my body like the wheel of a car. Too bad. I should have to resign myself; I could live with only one leg. The main thing was not to think about it. Above all, not at this moment. Leave thoughts for later.

Our march had lost all semblance of discipline. We went as we wanted, as we could. We heard no more shots. Our guards must have been tired.

But death scarcely needed any help from them. The cold was conscientiously doing its work. At every step someone fell and suffered no more.

From time to time, SS officers on motorcycles would go down the length of the column to try and shake us out of our growing apathy:

"Keep going! We are getting there!"

"Courage! Only a few more hours!"

"We're reaching Gleiwitz."

These words of encouragement, even though they came from the mouths of our assassins, did us a great deal of good. No one wanted to give up now, just before the end, so near to the goal. Our eyes searched the horizon for the barbed wire of Gleiwitz. Our only desire was to reach it as quickly as possible.

The night had now set in. The snow had ceased to fall. We walked for several more hours before arriving.

We did not notice the camp until we were just in front of the gate.

Some Kapos rapidly installed us in the barracks. We pushed and jostled one another as if this were the supreme refuge, the gateway to life. We walked over pain-racked bodies. We trod on wounded faces. No cries. A few groans. My father and I were ourselves thrown to the ground by this rolling tide. Beneath our feet someone let out a rattling cry:

"You're crushing me . . . mercy!"

A voice that was not unknown to me.

"You're crushing me . . . mercy! mercy!"

The same faint voice, the same rattle, heard somewhere before. That voice had spoken to me one day. Where? When? Years ago? No, it could only have been at the camp.

"Mercy!"

I felt that I was crushing him. I was stopping his breath. I wanted to get up. I struggled to disengage myself, so that he could breathe. But I was crushed myself beneath the weight of other bodies. I could hardly breathe. I dug my nails into unknown faces. I was biting all round me, in order to get air. No one cried out.

Suddenly I remembered. Juliek! The boy from Warsaw who played the violin in the band at Buna. . . .

"Juliek, is it you?"

"Eliezer . . . the twenty-five strokes of the whip. Yes . . . I remember."

He was silent. A long moment elapsed.

"Juliek! Can you hear me, Juliek?"

"Yes . . .," he said, in a feeble voice. "What do you want?"

He was not dead.

"How do you feel, Juliek?" I asked, less to know the answer than to hear that he could speak, that he was alive.

"All right, Eliezer. . . . I'm getting on all right . . . hardly any air . . . worn out. My feet are swollen. It's good to rest, but my violin. . . ."

I thought he had gone out of his mind. What use was the violin here?

"What, your violin?"

He gasped.

"I'm afraid . . . I'm afraid . . . that they'll break my violin. . . . I've brought it with me."

I could not answer him. Someone was lying full length on top of me, covering my face. I was unable to breathe, through either mouth or nose. Sweat beaded my brow, ran down my spine. This was the end—the end of the road. A silent death, suffocation. No way of crying out, of calling for help.

I tried to get rid of my invisible assassin. My whole will to live was centered in my nails. I scratched. I battled for a mouthful of air. I tore at decaying flesh which did not respond. I could not free myself from this mass weighing down my chest. Was it a dead man I was struggling against? Who knows?

I shall never know. All I can say is that I won. I succeeded in digging a hole through this wall of dying people, a little hole through which I could drink in a small quantity of air.

"Father, how are you?" I asked, as soon as I could utter a word.

I knew he could not be far from me.

"Well!" answered a distant voice, which seemed to come from another world. I tried to sleep.

He tried to sleep. Was he right or wrong? Could one sleep here? Was it not dangerous to allow your vigilance to fail, even for a moment, when at any minute death could pounce upon you?

I was thinking of this when I heard the sound of a violin. The sound of a violin, in this dark shed, where the dead were heaped on the living. What madman could be playing the violin here, at the brink of his own grave? Or was it really an hallucination?

It must have been Juliek.

He played a fragment from Beethoven's concerto. I had never heard sounds so pure. In such a silence.

How had he managed to free himself? To draw his body from under mine without my being aware of it?

It was pitch dark. I could hear only the violin, and it was as though Juliek's soul were the bow. He was playing his life. The whole of his life was gliding on the strings—his lost hopes, his charred past, his extinguished future. He played as he would never play again.

I shall never forget Juliek. How could I forget that concert, given to an audience of dying and dead men! To this day, whenever I hear Beethoven played my eyes close and out of the dark rises the sad, pale face of my Polish friend, as he said farewell on his violin to an audience of dying men.

I do not know for how long he played. I was overcome by sleep. When I awoke, in the daylight, I could see Juliek, opposite me, slumped over, dead. Near him lay his violin, smashed, trampled, a strange overwhelming little corpse.

We stayed at Gleiwitz for three days. Three days without food or drink. We were not allowed to leave the barracks. SS men guarded the door.

I was hungry and thirsty. I must have been very dirty and exhausted, to judge from the appearance of the others. The bread we had brought from Buna had long since been devoured. And who knew when we would be given another ration?

The front was following us. We could hear new gun shots again, very close. But we had neither the strength nor the courage to believe that the Nazis would not have time to evacuate us, and that the Russians would soon be here.

We heard that we were going to be deported into the center of Germany.

On the third day, at dawn, we were driven out of the barracks. We all threw blankets over our shoulders, like prayer shawls. We were directed toward a gate which divided the camp into two. A group of SS officers were standing there. A rumor ran through our ranks—a selection!

The SS officers did the selecting. The weak, to the left; those who could walk well, to the right.

My father was sent to the left. I ran after him. An SS officer shouted at my back:

"Come back here!"

I slipped in among the others. Several SS rushed to bring me back, creating such confusion that many of the people from the left were able to come back to the right—and among them, my father and myself. However, there were some shots and some dead.

We were all made to leave the camp. After half an hour's marching we arrived right in the middle of a field divided by rails. We had to wait for the train to arrive.

The snow fell thickly. We were forbidden to sit down or even to move.

The snow began to form a thick layer over our blankets. They brought us bread—the usual ration. We threw ourselves upon it. Someone had the idea of appeasing his thirst by eating the snow. Soon the others were imitating him. As we were not allowed to bend down, everyone took out his spoon and ate the accumulated snow off his neighbor's back. A mouthful of bread and a spoonful of snow. The SS who were watching laughed at this spectacle.

Hours went by. Our eyes grew weary of scouring the horizon for the liberating train. It did not arrive until much later in the evening. An infinitely long train, composed of cattle wagons, with no roofs. The SS pushed us in, a hundred to a carriage, we were so thin! Our embarkation completed, the convoy set out.

Seven

Pressed up against the others in an effort to keep out the cold, head empty and heavy at the same time, brain a whirlpool of decaying memories. Indifference deadened the spirit. Here or elsewhere—what difference did it make? To die today or tomorrow, or later? The night was long and never ending.

When at last a gray glimmer of light appeared on the horizon, it revealed a tangle of human shapes, heads sunk upon shoulders, crouched, piled one on top of the other, like a field of dust-covered tombstones in the first light of the dawn. I tried to distinguish those who were still alive from those who had gone. But there was no difference. My gaze was held for a long time by one who lay with his eyes open, staring into the void. His livid face was covered with a layer of frost and snow.

My father was huddled near me, wrapped in his blanket, his shoulders covered with snow. And was he dead, too? I called him. No answer. I would have cried out if I could have done so. He did not move.

My mind was invaded suddenly by this realization—there was no more reason to live, no more reason to struggle.

The train stopped in the middle of a deserted field. The suddenness of the halt woke some of those who were asleep. They straightened themselves up, throwing startled looks around them.

Outside, the SS went by, shouting:

"Throw out all the dead! All corpses outside!"

The living rejoiced. There would be more room. Volunteers set to work. They felt those who were still crouching.

"Here's one! Take him!"

They undressed him, the survivors avidly sharing out his clothes, then two "gravediggers" took him, one by the head and one by the feet, and threw him out of the wagon like a sack of flour.

From all directions came cries:

"Come on! Here's one! This man next to me. He doesn't move."

I woke from my apathy just at the moment when two men came up to my father. I threw myself on top of his body. He was cold. I slapped him. I rubbed his hands, crying:

"Father! Father! Wake up. They're trying to throw you out of the carriage . . ."

His body remained inert.

The two gravediggers, seized me by the collar.

"Leave him. You can see perfectly well that he's dead."

"No!" I cried. "He isn't dead! Not yet!"

I set to work to slap him as hard as I could. After a moment my father's eyelids moved slightly over his glazed eyes. He was breathing weakly.

"You see," I cried.

The two men moved away.

Twenty bodies were thrown out of our wagon. Then the train resumed its journey, leaving behind it a few hundred naked dead, deprived of burial, in the deep snow of a field in Poland.

We were given no food. We lived on snow; it took the place of bread. The days were like nights, and the nights left the dregs of their darkness in our souls. The train was traveling slowly, often stopping for several hours and then setting off again. It never ceased snowing. All through these days and nights we stayed crouching, one on top of the other, never speaking a word. We were no more than frozen bodies. Our eyes closed, we waited merely for the next stop, so that we could unload our dead.

Ten days, ten nights of traveling. Sometimes we would pass through German townships. Very early in the morning, usually. The workmen were going to work. They stopped and stared after us, but otherwise showed no surprise.

One day when we had stopped, a workman took a piece of bread out of his bag and threw it into a wagon. There was a stampede. Dozens of starving men fought each other to the death for a few crumbs. The German workmen took a lively interest in this spectacle.

Some years later, I watched the same kind of scene at Aden. The passengers on our boat were amusing themselves by throwing coins to the "natives," who were diving in to get them. An attractive, aristocratic Parisienne was deriving special pleasure from the game. I suddenly noticed that two children were engaged in a death struggle, trying to strangle each other. I turned to the lady.

"Please," I begged, "don't throw any more money in!"

"Why not?" she said. "I like to give charity. . . ."

In the wagon where the bread had fallen, a real battle had broken out. Men threw themselves on top of each other, stamping on each other, tearing at each other, biting each other. Wild beasts of prey, with animal hatred in their eyes; an extraordinary vitality had seized them, sharpening their teeth and nails.

A crowd of workmen and curious spectators had collected along the train. They had probably never seen a train with such a cargo. Soon, nearly everywhere, pieces of bread were being dropped into the wagons. The audience stared at these skeletons of men, fighting one another to the death for a mouthful.

A piece fell into our wagon. I decided that I would not move. Anyway, I knew that I would never have the strength to fight with a dozen savage men! Not far away I noticed an old man dragging himself along on all fours. He was trying to disengage himself from the struggle. He held one hand to his heart. I thought at first he had received a blow in the chest. Then I understood; he had a bit of bread under his shirt. With remarkable speed he drew it out and put it to his mouth. His eyes gleamed; a smile, like a grimace, lit up his dead face. And was immediately extinguished. A shadow had just loomed up near him. The shadow threw itself upon him. Felled to the ground, stunned with blows, the old man cried:

"Meir. Meir, my boy! Don't you recognize me? I'm your father . . . you're hurting me . . . you're killing your father! I've got some bread . . . for you too . . . for you too. . . ."

He collapsed. His fist was still clenched around a small piece. He tried to carry it to his mouth. But the other one threw himself upon him and snatched it. The old man again whispered something, let out a rattle, and died amid the general indifference. His son searched him, took the bread, and began to devour it. He was not able to get very far. Two men had seen and hurled themselves upon him. Others joined in. When they withdrew, next to me were two corpses, side by side, the father and the son.

I was fifteen years old.

In our wagon, there was a friend of my father's called Meir Katz. He had worked as a gardener at Buna and used to bring us a few green vegetables occasionally. Being less undernourished than the rest of us, he had stood up to imprisonment better. Because he was relatively more vigorous, he had been put in charge of the wagon.

On the third night of our journey I woke up suddenly and felt two hands on my throat, trying to strangle me. I just had the time to shout, "Father!"

Nothing but this word. I felt myself suffocating. But my father had woken up and seized my attacker. Too weak to overcome him, he had the idea of calling Meir Katz.

"Come here! Come quickly! There's someone strangling my son."

A few moments later I was free. I still do not know why the man wanted to strangle me.

After a few days, Meir Katz spoke to my father:

"Chlomo, I'm getting weak. I'm losing my strength. I can't hold on. . . ."

"Don't let yourself go under," my father said, trying to encourage him. "You must resist. Don't lose faith in yourself."

But Meir Katz groaned heavily in reply.

"I can't go on any longer, Chlomo! What can I do? I can't carry on. . . ."

My father took his arm. And Meir Katz, the strong man, the most robust of us all, wept. His son had been taken from him at the time of the first selection, but it was now that he wept. It was now that he cracked up. He was finished, at the end of his tether.

On the last day of our journey a terrible wind arose; it snowed without ceasing. We felt that the end was near—the real end. We could never hold out in this icy wind, in these gusts.

Someone got up and shouted:

"We mustn't stay sitting down at a time like this. We shall freeze to death! Let's all get up and move a bit. . . ."

We all got up. We held our damp blankets more tightly around us. And we forced ourselves to move a few steps, to turn around where we were.

Suddenly a cry rose up from the wagon, the cry of a wounded animal. Someone had just died.

Others, feeling that they too were about to die, imitated his cry. And their cries seemed to come from beyond the grave. Soon everyone was crying out. Wailing, groaning, cries of distress hurled into the wind and the snow.

The contagion spread to the other carriages. Hundreds of cries rose up simultaneously. Not knowing against whom we cried. Not knowing why. The death rattle of a whole convoy who felt the end upon them. We were all going to die here. All limits had been passed. No one had any strength left. And again the night would be long.

Meir Katz groaned:

"Why don't they shoot us all right away?"

That same evening, we reached our destination.

It was late at night. The guards came to unload us. The dead were abandoned in the train. Only those who could still stand were able to get out.

Meir Katz stayed in the train. The last day had been the most murderous. A hundred of us had got into the wagon. A dozen of us got out—among them, my father and I.

We had arrived at Buchenwald.

Eight

AT THE GATE OF THE CAMP, SS officers were waiting for us. They counted us. Then we were directed to the assembly place. Orders were given us through loudspeakers:

"Form fives!" "Form groups of a hundred!" "Five paces forward!"

I held onto my father's hand—the old, familiar fear: not to lose him.

Right next to us the high chimney of the crematory oven rose up. It no longer made any impression on us. It scarcely attracted our attention.

An established inmate of Buchenwald told us that we should have a shower and then we could go into the blocks. The idea of having a hot bath fascinated me. My father was silent. He was breathing heavily beside me.

"Father," I said. "Only another moment more. Soon we can lie down—in a bed. You can rest. . . ."

He did not answer. I was so exhausted myself that his silence left me indifferent. My only wish was to take a bath as quickly as possible and lie down in a bed.

But it was not easy to reach the showers. Hundreds of prisoners were crowding there. The guards were unable to keep any order. They struck out right and left with no apparent result. Others, without the strength to push or even to stand up, had sat down in the snow. My father wanted to do the same. He groaned.

"I can't go on. . . . This is the end. . . . I'm going to die here. . . . "

He dragged me toward a hillock of snow from which emerged human shapes and ragged pieces of blanket.

"Leave me," he said to me. "I can't go on. . . . Have mercy on me. . . . I'll wait here until we can get into the baths. . . . You can come and find me."

I could have wept with rage. Having lived through so much, suffered so much, could I leave my father to die now? Now, when we could have a good hot bath and lie down?

"Father!" I screamed. "Father! Get up from here! Immediately! You're killing yourself. . . ."

I seized him by the arm. He continued to groan.

"Don't shout, son. . . . Take pity on your old father. . . . Leave me to rest here . . . just for a bit, I'm so tired . . . at the end of my strength. . . ."

He had become like a child, weak, timid, vulnerable.

"Father," I said. "You can't stay here."

I showed him the corpses all around him; they too had wanted to rest here.

"I can see them, son. I can see them all right. Let them sleep. It's so long since they closed their eyes. . . . They are exhausted . . . exhausted. . . ."

His voice was tender.

I yelled against the wind:

"They'll never wake again! Never! Don't you understand?"

For a long time this argument went on. I felt that I was not arguing with him, but with death itself, with the death that he had already chosen.

The sirens began to wail. An alert. The lights went out throughout the camp. The guards drove us toward the blocks. In a flash, there was no one left on the assembly place. We were only too glad not to have had to stay outside longer in the icy wind. We let ourselves sink down onto the planks. The beds were in several tiers. The cauldrons of soup at the entrance attracted no one. To sleep, that was all that mattered.

It was daytime when I awoke. And then I remembered that I had a father. Since the alert, I had followed the crowd without troubling about him. I had known that he was at the end, on the brink of death, and yet I had abandoned him.

I went to look for him.

But at the same moment this thought came into my mind: "Don't let me find him! If only I could get rid of this dead weight, so that I could use all my strength to struggle for my own survival, and only worry about myself." Immediately I felt ashamed of myself, ashamed forever.

I walked for hours without finding him. Then I came to the block where they were giving out black "coffee." The men were lining up and fighting.

A plaintive, beseeching voice caught me in the spine:

"Eliezer . . . my son . . . bring me . . . a drop of coffee. . . ."

I ran to him.

"Father! I've been looking for you for so long. . . . Where were you? Did you sleep? . . . How do you feel?"

He was burning with fever. Like a wild beast, I cleared a way for myself to the coffee cauldron. And I managed to carry back a cupful. I had a sip. The rest was for him. I can't forget the light of thankfulness in his eyes while he gulped it down—an animal gratitude. With those few gulps of hot water, I probably brought him more satisfaction than I had done during my whole childhood.

He was lying on a plank, livid, his lips pale and dried up, shaken by tremors. I could not stay by him for long. Orders had been given to clear the place for cleaning. Only the sick could stay.

We stayed outside for five hours. Soup was given out. As soon as we were allowed to go back to the blocks, I ran to my father.

"Have you had anything to eat?"

"No."

"Why not?"

"They didn't give us anything . . . they said that if we were ill we should die soon anyway and it would be a pity to waste the food. I can't go on any more. . . ."

I gave him what was left of my soup. But it was with a heavy heart. I felt that I was giving it up to him against my will. No better than Rabbi Eliahou's son had I withstood the test.

He grew weaker day by day, his gaze veiled, his face the color of dead leaves. On the third day after our arrival at Buchenwald, everyone had to go to the showers. Even the sick, who had to go through last.

On the way back from the baths, we had to wait outside for a long time. They had not yet finished cleaning the blocks.

Seeing my father in the distance, I ran to meet him. He went by me like a ghost, passed me without stopping, without looking at me. I called to him. He did not come back. I ran after him:

"Father, where are you running to?"

He looked at me for a moment, and his gaze was distant, visionary; it was the face of someone else. A moment only and on he ran again.

Struck down with dysentery, my father lay in his bunk, five other invalids with him. I sat by his side, watching him, not daring to believe that he could escape death again. Nevertheless, I did all I could to give him hope.

Suddenly, he raised himself on his bunk and put his feverish lips to my ear:

"Eliezer . . . I must tell you where to find the gold and the money I buried . . . in the cellar. . . . You know. . . ."

He began to talk faster and faster, as though he were afraid he would not have time to tell me. I tried to explain to him that this was not the end, that we would go back to the house together, but he would not listen to me. He could no longer listen to me. He was exhausted. A trickle of saliva, mingled with blood, was running from between his lips. He had closed his eyes. His breath was coming in gasps.

For a ration of bread, I managed to change beds with a prisoner in my father's bunk. In the afternoon the doctor came. I went and told him that my father was very ill.

"Bring him here!"

I explained that he could not stand up. But the doctor refused to listen to anything. Somehow, I brought my father to him. He stared at him, then questioned him in a clipped voice:

"What do you want?"

"My father's ill," I answered for him. "Dysentery."

"Dysentery? That's not my business. I'm a surgeon. Go on! Make room for the others."

Protests did no good.

"I can't go on, son. . . . Take me back to my bunk. . . ."

I took him back and helped him to lie down. He was shivering.

"Try and sleep a bit, father. Try to go to sleep."

His breathing was labored, thick. He kept his eyes shut. Yet I was convinced that he could see everything, that now he could see the truth in all things.

Another doctor came to the block. But my father would not get up. He knew that it was useless.

Besides, this doctor had only come to finish off the sick. I could hear him shouting at them that they were lazy and just wanted to stay in bed. I felt like leaping at his throat, strangling him. But I no longer had the courage or the strength. I was riveted to my father's deathbed. My hands hurt, I was clenching them so hard. Oh, to strangle the doctor and the others! To burn the whole world! My father's murderers! But the cry stayed in my throat.

When I came back from the bread distribution, I found my father weeping like a child:

"Son, they keep hitting me!"

"Who?"

I thought he was delirious.

"Him, the Frenchman . . . and the Pole . . . they were hitting me."

Another wound to the heart, another hate, another reason for living lost.

"Eliezer . . . Eliezer . . . tell them not to hit me. . . . I haven't done anything. . . . Why do they keep hitting me?"

I began to abuse his neighbors. They laughed at me. I promised them bread, soup. They laughed. Then they got angry; they could not stand my father any longer, they said, because he was now unable to drag himself outside to relieve himself.

The following day he complained that they had taken his ration of bread.

"While you were asleep?"

"No. I wasn't asleep. They jumped on top of me. They snatched my bread . . . and they hit me . . . again. . . . I can't stand any more, son . . . a drop of water. . . ."

I knew that he must not drink. But he pleaded with me for so long that I gave in. Water was the worst poison he could have, but what else could I do for him? With water, without water, it would all be over soon anyway. . . .

"You, at least, have some mercy on me. . . ."

Have mercy on him! I, his only son!

A week went by like this.

"This is your father, isn't it?" asked the head of the block.

"Yes."

"He's very ill."

"The doctor won't do anything for him."

"The doctor can't do anything for him, now. And neither can you."

He put his great hairy hand on my shoulder and added:

"Listen to me, boy. Don't forget that you're in a concentration camp. Here, every man has to fight for himself and not think of anyone else. Even of his father. Here, there are no fathers, no brothers, no friends. Everyone lives and dies for himself alone. I'll give you a sound piece of advice—don't give your ration of bread and soup to your old father. There's nothing you can do for him. And you're killing yourself. Instead, you ought to be having his ration."

I listened to him without interrupting. He was right, I thought in the most secret region of my heart, but I dared not admit it. It's too late to save your old father, I said to myself. You ought to be having two rations of bread, two rations of soup. . . .

Only a fraction of a second, but I felt guilty. I ran to find a little soup to give my father. But he did not want it. All he wanted was water.

"Don't drink water . . . have some soup."

"I'm burning . . . why are you being so unkind to me, my son? Some water. . . ."

I brought him some water. Then I left the block for roll call. But I turned around and came back again. I lay down on the top bunk. Invalids were allowed to stay in the block. So I would be an invalid myself. I would not leave my father.

There was silence all round now, broken only by groans. In front of the block, the SS were giving orders. An officer passed by the beds. My father begged me:

"My son, some water. . . . I'm burning. . . . My stomach. . . ."

"Quiet, over there !" yelled the officer.

"Eliezer," went on my father, "some water. . . ."

The officer came up to him and shouted at him to be quiet. But my father did not hear him. He went on calling me. The officer dealt him a violent blow on the head with his truncheon.

I did not move. I was afraid. My body was afraid of also receiving a blow.

Then my father made a rattling noise and it was my name: "Eliezer."

I could see that he was still breathing—spasmodically.

I did not move.

When I got down after roll call, I could see his lips trembling as he murmured something. Bending over him, I stayed gazing at him for over an hour, engraving into myself the picture of his bloodstained face, his shattered skull.

Then I had to go to bed. I climbed into my bunk, above my father, who was still alive. It was January 28, 1945.

I awoke on January 29 at dawn. In my father's place lay another invalid. They must have taken him away before dawn and carried him to the crematory. He may still have been breathing.

There were no prayers at his grave. No candles were lit to his memory. His last word was my name. A summons, to which I did not respond.

I did not weep, and it pained me that I could not weep. But I had no more tears. And, in the depths of my being, in the recesses of my weakened conscience, could I have searched it, I might perhaps have found something like—free at last!

Nine

I HAD TO STAY at Buchenwald until April eleventh. I have nothing to say of my life during this period. It no longer mattered. After my father's death, nothing could touch me any more.

I was transferred to the children's block, where there were six hundred of us. The front was drawing nearer.

I spent my days in a state of total idleness. And I had but one desire—to eat. I no longer thought of my father or of my mother.

From time to time I would dream of a drop of soup, of an extra ration of soup. . . .

On April fifth, the wheel of history turned.

It was late in the afternoon. We were standing in the block, waiting for an SS man to come and count us. He was late in coming. Such a delay was unknown till then in the history of Buchenwald. Something must have happened.

Two hours later the loudspeakers sent out an order from the head of the camp: all the Jews must come to the assembly place.

This was the end! Hitler was going to keep his promise.

The children in our block went toward the place. There was nothing else we could do. Gustav, the head of the block, made this clear to us with his truncheon. But on the way we met some prisoners who whispered to us:

"Go back to your block. The Germans are going to shoot you. Go back to your block, and don't move."

We went back to our block. We learned on the way that the camp resistance organization had decided not to abandon the Jews and was going to prevent their being liquidated.

As it was late and there was great upheaval—innumerable Jews had passed themselves off as non-Jews—the head of the camp decided that a general roll call would take place the following day. Everybody would have to be present.

The roll call took place. The head of the camp announced that Buchenwald was to be liquidated. Ten blocks of deportees would be evacuated each day. From this moment, there would be no further distribution of bread and soup. And the evacuation began. Every day, several thousand prisoners went through the camp gate and never came back.

On April tenth, there were still about twenty thousand of us in the camp, including several hundred children. They decided to evacuate us all at once, right on until the evening. Afterward, they were going to blow up the camp.

So we were massed in the huge assembly square, in rows of five, waiting to see the gate open. Suddenly, the sirens began to wail. An alert! We went back to the blocks. It was too late to evacuate us that evening. The evacuation was postponed again to the following day.

We were tormented with hunger. We had eaten nothing for six days, except a bit of grass or some potato peelings found near the kitchens.

At ten o'clock in the morning the SS scattered through the camp, moving the last victims toward the assembly place.

Then the resistance movement decided to act. Armed men suddenly rose up everywhere. Bursts of firing. Grenades exploding. We children stayed flat on the ground in the block.

The battle did not last long. Toward noon everything was quiet again. The SS had fled and the resistance had taken charge of the running of the camp.

At about six o'clock in the evening, the first American tank stood at the gates of Buchenwald.

Our first act as free men was to throw ourselves onto the provisions. We thought only of that. Not of revenge, not of our families. Nothing but bread.

And even when we were no longer hungry, there was still no one who thought of revenge. On the following day, some of the young men went to Weimar to get some potatoes and clothes—and to sleep with girls. But of revenge, not a sign.

Three days after the liberation of Buchenwald I became very ill with food poisoning. I was transferred to the hospital and spent two weeks between life and death.

One day I was able to get up, after gathering all my strength, I wanted to see myself in the mirror hanging on the opposite wall. I had not seen myself since the ghetto.

From the depths of the mirror, a corpse gazed back at me.

The look in his eyes, as they stared into mine, has never left me.

Related Readings

Continued

Related Readings *Continued*

Bob Costas

A Wound That Will Never Be Healed:

An Interview with Elie Wiesel

NBC broadcaster Bob Costas sat down for a one-on-one interview with Night *author Elie Wiesel. This transcript of that interview provides additional information about* Night.

BC: How would you describe Sighet, your childhood home, and what was your childhood like before you were taken from there?

EW: It was a typical *shtetl*, meaning a typical Jewish town. Majority Jewish. Fifteen thousand Jews, some ten thousand non-Jews, but the life was dominated by the Jews, meaning on Saturday, all the shops were closed. On Jewish holidays, even the non-Jews participated somehow in those holidays. My childhood was a happy/unhappy childhood. Happy because I was home with my family, with my teachers, my friends. Profoundly religious. I was profoundly religious, meaning, to me, God was more important than any other person in the world. I was obsessed with it, with study, with prayer—fanatically obsessed. Today, when I think about it, I'm inundated with sadness. I didn't know, for instance, how poor the poor Jews were. Because we had our wealthy people, our poor people; we had people who were bourgeois,[1] those

---

1. **bourgeois** middle class

who were very rich. And then when I came back twenty years later, I realized that even the rich were very poor. And yet, it came on a *Shabbat*, on a Saturday, the poverty was gone. People who were coachmen, who were cobblers, tailors, who had difficulties making a living during the week, but the moment the Saturday set in, the Sabbath set in, we had the feeling that a strange metamorphosis occurred, that the profane became sacred.

BC: As Hitler's Gestapo went about its work and reports filtered into that part of Transylvania about the atrocities that were going on nearby, most people, for one reason or another, according to what I've read of your writings, didn't believe it. Even when a gentlemen known as Moché the Beadle² came back, having escaped, and tried to warn them, they thought he was mad, right?

EW: Yes. That happened in 1941. The Hungarians were then in control, in power. And in 1941, they decided to deport the so-called foreign Jews, foreign-born Jews. And they were not foreign-born, not more than I, no more than I, but yet they couldn't prove that they were citizens. And they were deported across the border to Galicia, and they were all killed—machine-gunned—and only one escaped, this Moché the Beadle. And he came back. And I loved him. I loved stories, and I loved his stories, too. They were horrible stories, but I loved them anyway. But nobody believed him. Why should they have believed him? He was not an important person, he was a beadle. And everybody was convinced that he had lost his mind. And then he stopped talking altogether because nobody believed him. Therefore, I am so angry at people who knew and didn't tell us. If we had heard—let's say in 1943, even after the Warsaw Ghetto uprising—if we had heard a broadcast by Roosevelt, by Churchill, or by Jewish leaders in Palestine then, or in America, I think we would have taken it seriously. But to take seriously a beadle? Hallucinations. And as a result, when we came in 1944 to Auschwitz, we didn't know what it meant.

BC: So when they first gathered you up and took you from your home, were you actually hopeful? Could you rationalize some possibility, some outcome here, other than death, other than this unthinkable outcome?

EW: We didn't think of death. It happened in March—March 19, 1944, the Germans came into Hungary. Two months or so before the Normandy invasion. The Russians were very near. And then the ghetto arrived. Two weeks later, we were all in the ghetto. At night we would see the artillery exchange between the Russians and the Germans. They were only twenty kilometers

---

2. **beadle** minor official in a synagogue

away. We could have escaped. There was nothing to prevent us from escaping because there were two Germans, Eichmann and someone else, some fifty Hungarian gendarmes,[3] and there was no problem. We could have left the ghetto into the mountains. We had non-Jewish friends who wanted us to come and stay with them. But we didn't know. We thought the war would end soon, and the Russians would come in, and Hitler would be defeated, and everything would come back to normalcy.

BC: When they loaded you all up and took you out of town, did you think then that this was the end of the line, or did you think that perhaps you would simply be detained for a while and, when the war ended, liberated?

EW: Well, the Germans had developed a psychology, a kind of mass psychology, how to fool, how to deceive the victims. And we were all victims. We didn't know. Until the very last moment, we believed that families would remain together, and we should be in some labor camp. Young people would work, and the parents would stay home and prepare food, meals. We didn't know until the very last minute, until it was too late.

BC: I know that you'll never forget the words "Men to the left, women to the right." That's how they separated you from your mother and your sisters, you and your father.

EW: Well, of course, that was the real shock, the brutality of the words. The words were simple, "left" and "right," but what they meant, the meaning of those words, hit me much later. For three days or so I was in a haze. I thought I was dreaming. For three days I was dreaming. We were there in the shadow of the flames, and to me it wasn't real. I couldn't believe it. I write about it in *Night*. I couldn't believe it that in the twentieth century, in the middle of the twentieth century, people should do that, could do that, to other people. I somehow couldn't accept it, and to this day I cannot accept it. Something in me rejects that notion that would dehumanize a killer to such an extent. And the complicity, the indifference of the world—this, to this day, it moves me to anger.

BC: When they tattooed a number on your arm, was that the single most dehumanizing moment, or is it just one in a litany[4] of dehumanizing moments?

EW: Oh, that didn't mean a thing, but the first dehumanizing incident was the day when we arrived, really. (I mean the next day—we arrived at

---

3. **gendarmes** police officers
4. **litany** list

night.) And there was a Kapo, and my father went to him saying he would like to go to the toilet. And my father was a respectful man. And the Kapo hit him in his face, and my father fell to the ground. That was the beginning of the experience really, that I, his only son, couldn't come to his help. Usually I should have thrown myself at the tormentor and beat him up. But that was the first realization there that he and I were already in prison, and not only I, but my mind is in prison, my soul is in prison, my being is in prison, and I am no longer free to do what I want to do.

BC: Was there talk from time to time of inmates banding together in some kind of revolt which, even if it were to fail, at least would have liberated their spirits from captivity?

EW: There were revolts even at Buchenwald. The *Sonderkommando*, the commander that burned the corpses, that staged the revolt in 1944, they were all killed afterwards. In our camps, both in Auschwitz-Birkenau, where I was, and then Buchenwald, there were members of the resistance. I know that, but I was so young, and I was so timid, that I didn't even know about it. I knew vaguely that some people are members of an underground organization because they hanged a few.

BC: What were the most conspicuous examples of heroism, under the circumstances, that you saw, and were there examples of cowardice that you saw among the captive Jews?

EW: Cowardice is a word that we didn't apply because, logically, everyone should have been a coward—could have been and probably was because one SS[5] man with a machine gun was stronger than a thousand poets. Heroism . . . I've seen heroism, a spectacular kind of heroism, which I described when three members of the underground were hanged, and the way they faced the execution was heroic. But then I've seen heroism in a simple way. Let's say a man who would come to us on the Sabbath—I don't even know his name—and would simply say, "Don't forget that today is *Shabbat*." Don't forget that today is Sabbath. To us it meant nothing, because how could it? Same thing, Sabbath, Sunday, Monday. We were all destined to be killed. The fact that he said, "Don't forget that it is the Sabbath, a sacred day." Or somebody would come and say, "Don't forget your name. You are not only a number, you have a name." I've seen people giving their bread to their comrades whom they didn't know. I've seen a person who has offered himself to be beaten up instead of somebody else,

---

5. **SS** Corps of German troops organized by Hitler in the 1920s as his personal bodyguard and later put in charge of exterminations and massacres in conquered countries. Abbreviation for *schutzstaffel,* or protection staff.

whom he didn't know. In general, you know, the enemy, the killers, what they wanted to do there was to dehumanize the victim by depriving him of all moral values. Therefore the first lesson that they gave us was you are alone; don't count on anyone, don't think of anyone, only of yourself. You are alone, and only you should matter to yourself. And they were wrong. Because those who did care for somebody else—a father for his father, a son for his father, a friend for a friend—I think they lived longer because they felt committed, which means humanity became heroic in their own hearts.

BC: As I said, you and your father were separated, as they broke the men and the women apart, from your mother and your sisters, and you would never see your younger sister or your mother again; they perished. The theme of *Night* (your first book) that runs through the whole thing is your father trying to support you, you trying to support your father, at all costs not becoming separated from each other. And then just one of the tragic facts of those years is that your father finally succumbed only months before the U.S. forces liberated the concentration camp.

EW: As long as my father was alive, I was alive. When he died, I was no longer alive. It wasn't life; it was something else. I existed, but I didn't live. And even when we were together we had a certain code. We didn't talk about my mother, my sisters. We didn't talk. We were afraid. There were certain things in those times and in those places that people cannot understand today. We didn't cry. People didn't cry inside that universe. Maybe because people were afraid if they were to start crying, they would never end. But people didn't cry. Even when there were selections and somebody left somebody else, there were no tears. It was something so harsh—the despair was so harsh—that it didn't dissolve itself in tears, or in prayers either.

BC: You saw the reverse, though, too. I mean, you detail situations where a son beat his father because that was the way he thought, at least temporarily, to get into the good graces of his captors; a situation where a younger, stronger son took a morsel of bread from his dying father.

EW: Yes, I've seen, but there were very few, really, in truth, there were few. It's normal. But what happened there, the killers managed to create a universe parallel to our own. The kind of creation, a parallel creation, and there they established their own society with its own rulers, with its own philosophers, its own psychologists, its own poets, with a new society outside God, outside humanity. And, naturally, some succumbed. I cannot even judge them. I cannot be angry at them. Imagine a child of twelve arriving in Auschwitz, and he knows that only violence could be a refuge. Either he becomes an author of violence or a victim of violence. So, a child of twelve overnight aged and became an old person. How can I judge such a child? He didn't do it. He was made to do it by—he was conditioned to do it—by the tormentor. If I am angry, I am angry at the tormentor, not at the victim.

BC: Toward the end of *Night*, you describe your father's death. And he did not go to the furnaces, except to burn his corpse. He died of dysentery[6] and a combination of the hardships.

EW: The hunger. Hunger and exhaustion, fatigue.

BC: And the last night, he was calling out to you for water, but at the same time a guard was beating him. And your best judgment was that you couldn't help him. You were helpless; you didn't respond. And then you write, "There were no prayers at his grave. No candles were lit to his memory. His last word was my name. A summons to which I did not respond." You couldn't possibly feel guilt about that, if you are being hard on yourself.

EW: I do, I do. I do feel guilt. I know that logically I shouldn't, but I do feel guilty because we were terribly close. We became very close there. But, at the same time, the instinct prevented me from being killed. If I had moved, I would have been killed. Beaten up to death. I was as weak as he was. And who would have known that he would die that night? And we didn't know. But I do feel guilty.

BC: You saw a child, who you described as having the face of an angel—saw that child hanged. That's one of the most moving passages in the book. This is (obviously you have steeled yourself) your life's work, to tell of these things, so that's why I feel no reluctance to ask you to tell again, but how does somebody watch these things—these things unthinkable if we read them in fiction—unfold and then find some reason to keep on living?

EW: Well, first, you know, I don't speak about this often. I have written a few books, very few. I prefer, I think, books on the Talmud[7] and the Bible. And through them, I transmit certain obsessions, certain fears, or certain memories. At that time it was my father who kept me alive. We saw it together. And I wanted him to live. I knew that if I die, he will die. And that was the reason I could eat after having seen that scene, the hanging.

---

6. **dysentery** intestinal disorder characterized by severe diarrhea.
7. **Talmud** collection of Jewish civil and canonical law

And I remember it well, I remember it now. I didn't forget a single instant, a single episode.

BC: Did you assume, as you and your father tried as best you could to survive, that your mother and your sister were dead?

EW: Oh, we knew, but we didn't talk about it. I knew. He knew. At one point only, the very first night, when we were walking toward the flames—we didn't know yet anything, but we were walking toward the flames—my father said, "Maybe you should have gone with your mother." Had I gone with my mother, I would have been killed that night too. But we never talked about this. There was a kind of rule: we don't talk about it, about those who are absent, because it hurts too much. We couldn't accept such pain.

BC: Everyone, except those deranged and hateful souls who try to propound this preposterous theory that the Holocaust didn't occur, knows it occurred, and, statistically, they understand the dimensions of it. But until one hears the stories of Holocaust survivors and just a tiny number of the hundreds of thousands of particulars, until you hear that, you can't begin to grasp the ghastly horror of it. There is just no way, if you stood on a mountaintop for five thousand years and screamed to the top of your lungs, to overstate it.

EW: We cannot *overstate* it. We must *understate* it. To make it understandable, we must understate it. That's why in this little book, *Night*, which has few pages actually, what I *don't* say is important, as important as the things I *do* say. But even if you read all the books, all the documents, by all the survivors, you would still not know. Unfortunately, only those who were there know what it meant being there. And yet we try. One of my first goals, really, was to write for the survivors. I wanted them to write. In the beginning we didn't speak. Nobody spoke. We felt, who would understand? Who would believe? And why talk? And, really, the main reason for writing *Night* was not for the world or for history; it was for them. Look, it's important to bear witness. Important to tell your story. At the same time I know that even if all the stories were to be read by one person—the same person—you would still not know. You cannot imagine what it meant spending a night of death among death.

BC: Smelling burning flesh . . .

EW: The flames . . .

BC: . . . of being in the back of a wagon . . .

EW: . . . seeing . . .

BC: . . . with corpses . . .

EW: . . . seeing the flames . . .

BC: . . . all around you.

EW: . . . seeing the flames first of all, seeing the flames and smelling the smell. And knowing that it depends on the whim of an SS man. He didn't have to explain. Just capricious[8] gesture. And that's it.

BC: Did you ever see any humanity in the actions or in the eyes of your captors, any humanity at all?

EW: I did not.

BC: How do you suppose it is possible to purge humanity from so many people?

EW: Bob, this is the question of my life. After the war, I had a series of shocks, and one of the shocks was when I discovered that the commanders of the so-called *Einsatzkommando*, that did firing in Eastern Europe, meaning in the Ukraine and Russia, had college degrees. Some of them had Ph.D.s, and that, to me, an educator—I am a professor, I teach, I write—I can't understand it. What happened? Culture is supposed to be a shield, a moral shield. What happened to the shield? I don't understand that to this day.

BC: To murder children, to use them for bayonet practice in front of their parents.

EW: I don't understand that to this day. How is it possible? How come they didn't go mad? Morally mad if not mentally insane? But they did it, and for them it was a game. I am trying to understand this, so, I say to myself, maybe they tried to push the limits of cruelty farther and farther beyond the horizon. We are trying to push the limits of intelligence, of culture, of humanity, farther and farther, to broaden the scope, to broaden the realm of humanity, and they tried the opposite, which means they believed in a kind of God of evil. And, therefore, Hitler was a prophet of evil. And, therefore, they made an experiment. What can they obtain through evil? How far can they go in evil? But I don't understand.

BC: You came face to face with Dr. Joseph Mengele,[9] who wore a monocle,[10]

---

8. **capricious** impulsive or erratic

9. **Joseph Mengele** German war criminal; chief physician at Auschwitz, where he conducted cruel medical experiments on Jewish inmates and sent hundreds of thousands of Jews to their deaths

10. **monocle** eyeglass for one eye

carried a baton in his hand, an almost theatrical looking character. Can you describe him beyond that?

EW: He used to sing opera while he was doing what he was doing. He would sing melodies from opera. I heard it later on, really, from people who worked with him, inmates. He was an intelligent man, intellectual, polite. He even developed friendships with Jews, or with Gypsy children. There was a Gypsy camp, and he got fond of one of the Gypsy children, and his fondness then was translated in his own personal care of him: he took him to the gas chamber. The young Gypsy child whom he loved and caressed and embraced and kissed. I don't understand what happened to humanity, in the human being. I don't know.

BC: You mentioned that your life was a very religious life, devoted to the study of the Talmud. And you write of a point in this experience, where you say, "I was the accuser, God the accused. My eyes were open and I was alone—terribly alone in a world without God, and without man. Without love or mercy. I had ceased to be anything but ashes, yet, I felt myself to be stronger than the Almighty, to whom my life had been tied for so long. I stood amid a praying congregation, observing it like a stranger." You were spiritually and emotionally a dead person at the age of fifteen.

EW: But I kept on praying nevertheless. What I write here is a protest, and I believe in protest. I still believe in protest, even in protest against God. But what I felt then is true. But it was not a feeling of separation from God, meaning that I stopped believing in God. I protested against the injustice of God or the absence of God in the universe, in history. But even then I kept on believing.

BC: You never stopped believing?

EW: I had a crisis of faith after the war, not during. I came back, I came to France after the war. I reopened my religious life. I became as religious as before. And only later I began studying philosophy, and I worked, I worked in myself, and I had a crisis, a very serious crisis of faith.

BC: How long did it last, and how was it resolved?

EW: A few years. What saved me was my passion for study. I love to study. And even when I had a crisis, I kept on studying. It wasn't totally dissolved because even today I keep on asking questions, and there are no answers.

BC: A question which every kid with a high school education has heard, even one who's given scant thought to philosophy, is, if there is a God, how does God allow something like a Holocaust to happen?

EW: I don't know. If there is an answer, it is the wrong answer. But you see it's wrong, I think, to put everything on God's shoulders. That is something I understood later. Where was man? Where was humanity? Look, after all, we had faith in humanity—I had faith in humanity. To us, President Roosevelt was more important than Ben-Gurion.[11] I had never heard of the name of Ben-Gurion in my little town. But I knew the name of Roosevelt. I remember we said prayers for him. He was the father of the Jewish people. He knew. Absolutely he knew. And yet he refused to bomb the railways going to Auschwitz. Why? Had he done that—at that time, during the Hungarian deportation, ten thousand Jews were killed every day in Auschwitz. Even if the Germans had tried to repair the rail . . .

BC: So even as the U.S. waged war against the Axis powers, you're saying they didn't do enough to hit the specific targets. They could have stopped that cold.

EW: They could have. Look . . . they . . . I admire the American soldiers who fought Hitler, and I think we should be eternally grateful to them, to their families, to their children, to their parents. Many died in the war. They were heroes. But somehow the war that Hitler had waged against the Jewish people was forgotten. In the process. And that was wrong. A few bombing operations would have at least shown Hitler that the world cared. Hitler was convinced to the end that the world didn't care about what he and his acolytes[12] had done to the Jewish people.

BC: So even as the war turned against them and they were losing the war, almost to the last, they continued executing Jews. They continued their torture.

EW: Oh sure. Even at the end, trains carrying Jews to death had priority over military trains taking soldiers to the front. It was crazy. When you think about it, it's totally crazy. But that was their logic.

BC: Do you recall what you saw and what you felt the day the troops liberated Buchenwald in April of 1945?

EW: It was April 11, 1945, in the morning hours. We were the last remnants in Buchenwald, and I had been already at the gate almost every day. And, by accident, really, by chance, that the gate closed in front of me. So

---

11. **David Ben-Gurion** director of Jewish affairs in Palestine from 1935 to 1948
12. **acolytes** assistants

I came back to the camp. I remember when they came in. We were then already terribly hungry, more than usual because no food was given to us for six days, since April 5th. And I remember the first American soldiers. I remember black soldiers. I remember a black sergeant, huge. And then he saw us; he began sobbing and cursing. He was so moved by what he saw that he began sobbing—he sobbed like a child, and we couldn't console him. And we tried somehow to console him, and that made him sob even deeper, stronger, louder. So I remember those soldiers, and I have a weak— a soft spot—for the American soldier, really. I gave a lecture a few years ago at West Point, and it was amusing to me. I never had any military training or military affinity, and I came to give a lecture, and I told them what I felt about the American uniform, because that meant not only victory, it meant a triumph, the triumph of humanity. And to me, that black sergeant incarnates[13] that triumph.

BC: Toward the end of *Night*, you write about looking into a mirror. Apparently, you didn't have any access to a mirror for two years. What did you see when you looked into that mirror?

EW: Well, when the Americans came in they threw us food, and it was the wrong thing to do because they should have used medical supervision, and they didn't. And I remember I picked up a can, some dessert, something with ham in it. Now during the camp, I would have eaten anything, but I was already free, and my body knew it even before I did, and I put it to my lips and passed out, literally; I got some blood poisoning. So, I woke up in a hospital, a former SS hospital which was taken over by the Americans for inmates. So, I almost died. I was, I think, closer to death after the liberation than before. And then one day, really, I saw myself in that mirror. And I saw a person who was ageless, nameless, faceless. A person who belonged to another world, the world of the dead.

BC: If you belonged to the world of the dead (especially after your father slipped away from you only several weeks before the liberation came, which—the sad irony—just adds to the heartache), if you were dead inside at that point, from where did you summon the strength to direct a life so purposeful in the ensuing forty-plus years?

EW: In the beginning it was again, I repeat, a passion for study. I studied. I came to France together with four hundred youngsters, children, orphans, invited by DeGaulle. And we were taken over by an organization in a children's home, an orphans' home. And the first thing I did, when I came there, I asked for pen and paper. I began writing my memoirs. And for

---

13. **incarnates** signifies or symbolizes

quotations of the Talmud to study. It's later that I developed that since I am alive, I have to give meaning to my life. Oh, it may sound, you know, bombastic but it is true. That is how I switched. That means my life as it is, if it is only for myself, then it is wrong. I have to do something with it. I even have to do something with my memory of my death.

BC: **Apart from the physical horror, the murders, the torture, the hunger, the separation from loved ones, and then the ultimate loss of loved ones, is there any way to describe what it does to you psychologically to see people that you admire and respect rendered impotent and stripped of their identity, to see that all your mother could do for your little seven-year-old sister was to stroke her hair? That was all, in that circumstance, she could muster to protect her child.**

EW: That is a wound that will never be healed. But my father was helpless to protect me. That moment was to me probably the hardest in the entire period. Oh, I have seen professors, famous people, wealthy people, who had connections, who had a purpose in life, who had prestige, social status, and when they entered that universe they became objects like me. That is when I understood that something happened. A mutation. A mutation on the scale of being, that possessions meant nothing, what meant—I don't know what meant—violence. The choice really was to join the sadists, the executioner or to be, to remain, a victim.

BC: **And yet there were moments where humanity surfaced in such a shining, even if tragic, fashion. You mentioned the people going to the gallows without outward complaint and then, as a last word, saying, "Long live liberty." Or people volunteering to be beaten in place of another.**

EW: What a price. What a price, to die for a few words.

BC: **There is a passage here that is extraordinarily moving. There are a group of you loaded into a wagon, and many have died. It is a bitter winter, and there are sick people literally in amongst the corpses, in some cases being nearly smothered by the corpses. And there was a young man who had a violin.**

EW: Juliek.

BC: **"It was pitch dark. I could hear only the violin, and it was as though Juliek's soul were the bow. He was playing his life. The whole of his life was gliding on the strings—his lost hopes, his charred past, his extinguished future. He played as he would never play again. And of course this playing was banned." He could have been killed merely** for playing the violin. Especially for playing Beethoven on the violin, which the Germans found especially vile, coming from a Jew. I shall never forget him. "How could I forget that concert, given to an audience of dying and dead men! To this day, whenever I hear Beethoven played, my eyes close and out of the dark rises the sad, pale, face of my Polish friend, as he said farewell on his violin to an audience of dying men. I do not know for how long he played. I was overcome by sleep. When I awoke, in the daylight, I could see Juliek, opposite me, slumped over, dead. Near him lay his violin, smashed, trampled, a strange, overwhelming little corpse."

EW: You know, I used to play the violin before. I played well. And I haven't touched the violin since because of that.

BC: You were reunited with at least one sister, maybe two.

EW: Two.

BC: Two older sisters, by luck.

EW: Yeah, by luck. We were in that orphans' home, and after all four hundred children from Buchenwald, there was a story. The journalists came, and I had never seen a journalist in my life. I had never read the paper in my life. I didn't know who they were. And they spoke to me in German, and I answered in Yiddish. And they took a picture of me. I was playing chess with a friend, and a week later I was in the office of the director of that orphans' home. And I came to ask him about the Talmud. Had he received the book that I wanted? And I heard him speak on the telephone, mentioning my name. And I was too shy—I am a shy person. So I waited until he finished, and then I said, "Is it the Talmud?" He said, "What do you mean?" I said, "You were speaking about me." "Oh, no," he said, "your sister called." I said, "What? My sister? I don't have a sister." And then he realized—it's traumatic—he tried to call back, but they told him that the person who called had called from the post office because she didn't have a telephone. And he said, "She's waiting for you tomorrow in Paris." And for the whole day I was convinced it cannot be. And I came to Paris, and it was my oldest sister. She came to France with another man who was also in camp in Dachau, and they met after liberation, few days, and decided to get married. So she came with him to Paris. And one day she opened the paper; she saw my picture in it. And then we found the other sister, too, who went back to my hometown thinking maybe I was alive. And so, I met the two, and one of them died of cancer in the meantime. The middle one.

BC: There are too many things that have happened, even specific incidents, to touch on them all, but another ironic aspect to your life is that you are a free man; you are in New York City sometime in the '50s, I guess, and you are hit by a car.

EW: Yes.

BC: Thrown, or bounced around, by the impact for almost a block, your body broken, very near death, and somehow you came back from that experience as well.

EW: Oh, but that made me laugh, really. I wanted to laugh. To survive Auschwitz and die of an accident in New York was too much. It was a few weeks after I arrived. It was 1956. And I came in the evening to the New York Times to buy a paper and then to go and file a cable to the paper for which I worked, an Israeli paper, a very poor paper then. (Now it is very rich. Since I left it, it became rich.) And it, a taxi, ran over me. What seems today so unheard of, they brought me to the hospital (I think to one hospital; I won't mention it because otherwise they will sue you), and they checked my pockets, and they realized that I have no money and I am a refugee. They refused to take me. They put me back in the ambulance, and the ambulance went from one hospital to the other looking for a hospital that would take me. Finally they did go to the New York Hospital, and there the chief orthopedic surgeon, named Paul Braunstein, took me in, and he saved my life. I was days in a coma, and for a whole year, almost, I was in and out of hospitals.

BC: At that point was it possible to say to yourself—and this is so much easier for someone like me to theorize than for someone to do in the midst of the experiences that you've had—but did the thought cross your mind, "I'm some sort of superman?"

EW: No.

BC: "I'm here to overcome the obstacles?"

EW: Not really, not me. I'm not a superman. I was always, always weak and always shy, and I don't take initiatives. If I have to speak to somebody, I blush ten times. I am not that kind of person, really. That's why my sisters were convinced I died, because I was always sick when I was a child. And I would have been, really, the natural candidate for death. So, here too, oh, no, I felt it had to happen to me again, really.

BC: You have been involved in a number of humanitarian causes through the years, and that, combined with your writing, led to the

Nobel Prize for Peace in the mid-1980s and the single incident which most Americans would most associate you with: you come to the White House, President Reagan gives you a humanitarian award, but he's on his way in a few weeks to Bitburg to lay a wreath at the cemetery, and it's true that some Holocaust survivors, I guess, are buried there, but so too are officers of the SS.

EW: No Holocaust survivors there, only military, German military men, and SS people, SS men. Reagan—I have a soft spot for Reagan, too. He was a warm person, really. Except he relied too much on his advisors, and they told him to go. What I did, I sent him my speech beforehand—respect for the office of the President, after all. I sent him my speech. They behaved in the White House in a terrible way. I got the Congressional Gold Medal, which is the highest honor an American can get, you know. It's a very nice thing. And, by chance, the date was set for April 19. They could have had it in February, so the whole speech would not have taken place. Once they realized that Bitburg was coming, and I went to the White House without publicity, simply warning them, "Don't do it, because it will create a scandal," they didn't want to hear about it. Then, because of that, they decided to play low-key. And the ceremony was supposed to have taken place in the East Room, a hundred fifty people on my side, many members of Congress that I knew and friends, and a hundred fifty for the President. The last three days, three days before, they changed the room for the smallest room in the White House! And they hoped, you know, nobody would notice it and so forth. Little did they know it was going to be live broadcast on television and so forth. But I saw him even before. The day of the ceremony, I went to him, and I saw him, and I pleaded with him; I said, "Mr. President, don't do it. Don't go. You will be the hero. If, after my speech" (because you have to have the ceremony; you cannot go back on it) "you come and you say, 'Alright I'm not going,' you will be the hero all over the world." So one of his advisors said, "Yes, but not in Germany." I said, "So what? You go call up Chancellor Kohl and explain it to him. He will understand. You will make it up." But he didn't. And the funny part was, really, after my address they called me in, one of his senior advisors, senior staff members, that the President wants me to go with him, to go with him on Air Force One to Europe. And I thought that means he is not going to Bitburg, and my only concern was for my coming back: I have to teach in Boston, Boston University. So, I ask, "Alright, and then what?" He said, "You'll go to Bonn, and you'll go to Paris." I said, "And then what?" And he said, "You'll quickly go to Bitburg." I said, "What? I don't want *him* to go. You want *me* to go?" To show you that they didn't have the faintest notion of what the whole thing was about, the history in it.

BC: He thought, I guess, if you would accompany him, that it would be some sort of gesture of goodwill or reconciliation. He just didn't grasp the issues.

EW: The people around him—they had no idea of the historic implications, really.

BC: Then you saw him again, about a year later at the Ellis Island ceremonies, when they unveiled the new Statue of Liberty or the repaired Statue of Liberty?

EW: Then, there were, I think, ten or twelve foreign-born Americans who got these Liberty Medals. Kissinger,[14] myself, and Itzhak Perlman.[15] And it was awkward, a little bit, because once again he was giving me a medal. Different circumstances. It was nice anyway. It was a nice feeling.

BC: So you have no antagonism toward him?

EW: No, of course not. I feel for him. I feel sorry for him because it was the lowest point of his Presidency. And he could have avoided it. He deserves better than that, really, to remain in history linked to Bitburg.

BC: You had been to the Soviet Union in the mid-'60s, and you wrote a book called *The Jews of Silence*. Of course everyone knows at that time the circumstances: no possibility to emigrate, no possibility to openly practice their religion. Now a much different set of circumstances, and you saw Gorbachev[16] either very close to, or almost right in the middle of, the recent upheaval,[17] right?

EW: I saw him a few hours after he came back from his house arrest. I was sent there by President Francois Mitterand. He and I have been friends from before he was president. And he called me, and he gave me his presidential plane to go to Moscow and bring a personal message to Yeltsin[18] and Gorbachev of support and so forth. So I saw Gorbachev.

BC: What do you feel, in brief terms, is the future of Soviet Jewry?

EW: When I was there in '65, nobody knew about their tragedy. People

---

14. **Henry Kissinger** U.S. secretary of state from 1973 to 1977
15. **Itzhak Perlman** noted Israeli violinist
16. **Mikhail Gorbachev** political leader of Russia from 1985 to 1991; responsible for helping to end the Cold War
17. In an effort to block economic and social reforms in the Soviet Union, Communist Party leaders arrested then-President Mikhail Gorbachev in August 1991. Lacking popular support, the coup failed and the reforms continued.
18. **Boris Yeltsin** the first democratically elected Russian leader in history (1991)

didn't even know about their resistance. I was convinced I won't find Jews there—a few thousand Jews here and there. And when I came and I went to Kiev all I saw was fear, fear, fear. Everybody, but also Jewish fear. And then came a holiday called Simchath Torah, the Celebration of the Law, and I came to the synagogue in Moscow, and there were thousands and thousands and thousands of youngsters who came out with their musical instruments singing their allegiance to the Jewish people. And that was for me the beginning of the realization that they want to be Jewish, and they are free, they want to be free. Before Solzhenitsyn[19] and before Sakharov[20] and before the other dissidents, these youngsters defied the Kremlin and its terror. And so, then, I began really in '65 working for Soviet Jewry and the dissidents too, but they were the focus. I have faith in the Soviet Jews. I have faith in humanity in general in spite of everything else, and yet I have faith that many will leave, of course; many want to leave, but those who will remain will remain Jews.

BC: Did you ever, subsequent to Auschwitz, come face to face with Gestapo officers?

EW: No.

BC: Former Nazis? Not once?

EW: No. I came face to face, and I wrote about it in one of my books, in Israel, during the Eichmann[21] trial. I saw Eichmann at the trial, but he was in a glass cage. But later, I saw, in a bus, going from Tel Aviv to Jerusalem, a man that I—I recognized his neck. He was a kind of blockhouse, or barracks, head in Auschwitz. My barracks head. And I passed him, and all of a sudden I said, "Tell me, where were you during the war?" And he said, "Why?" And I said, "Aren't you a German Jew? Weren't you in Poland?" He said "Yes." "Weren't you in Auschwitz?" "Yes." "In the barracks?" "Yes." I gave him the number, at which point he paled because had I said, "You were a head of a barracks," they would have beaten him up during the Eichmann trial, and for a few seconds, I became his judge. Literally, I had his fate in my hands. And then, I decided, I am not a judge; I am a witness. I let him go.

BC: You understand, of course, the passion that fuels the work of so-called Nazi hunters. But your position has been different. Yours is to bear witness . . .

---

19. **Aleksandr Solzhenitsyn** Russian author and dissident
20. **Andrei Sakharov** Russian physicist and dissident
21. **Adolf Eichmann** Nazi official who coordinated the deportation of Jews in World War II

EW: Yes.

BC: . . . rather than to exact revenge or even pursue justice.

EW: Well, pursue justice, yes. But it's not my doing; I cannot do that. I admire those people who are doing it very well, and there are several of these young people, young people who dedicate their lives for the pursuit of justice, and all honor is due them. But my work is something else. I write. I teach. And I bear witness in my way. That doesn't mean I'm better, not at all, or worse. I don't think so. Except we all have our area of competence and activity.

BC: To you, what is happiness?

EW: A child.

BC: And yet you had no childhood. Once the Nazis came, you had no childhood anymore.

EW: Yes, but I was happy until then. I was very happy, meaning I knew the answers to all the questions. I knew I had a home. I had friends. I had teachers. I had God. I had happiness in my childhood. And, therefore, when I think of the past, what hurts most is when I think that a million Jewish children were killed, and since then, when I see a child, I go to pieces. Any child.

BC: What are your thoughts about your own son, who now is nearly twenty, I guess? When he was a small child, the innocence you saw in him must have been overwhelming.

EW: I'll tell you, my son and I have such a strange, marvelous, great relationship that he would not want me to speak about him. You will forgive me if I don't because he wouldn't like it.

BC: Is the God you believe in a God who exacts revenge?

EW: No, although we are told in the Psalms that God is a God of revenge. But I don't believe it. God is, as a philosopher said, God is patient. The whole problem of theodicy[22]—Why are the just punished and the wicked rewarded?—is answered in that line, that God is patient. What seems bad today, tomorrow is not so bad. And even if a person is happy today, the wicked person, tomorrow he won't be, or she won't be. So I don't think God is revengeful. God is truth. And when I speak of redemption in my books, it is the redemption of truths.

---

22. **theodicy** a defense of God's justice in permitting evil

BC: Do you believe in hell?

EW: Sure. Here, not there.

BC: So you don't believe, as some, I guess, would, that there is a hell where, literally or figuratively, a Hitler is consumed in flames.

EW: Oh, there are not enough flames for Hitler. Do I believe in the after-life? That's a different question, a difficult question—it's so complicated. You know, when does it begin? And who? And what? But I believe there is afterlife here, meaning a person can lead more than one life by committing himself or herself to certain causes. If I try to help another person, I think I would like to live his or her life or join my life to their life. So it is possible to have an afterlife even while being alive.

BC: Do you believe in the possibility, or at least hope for the possibility, of reconciliation with your father, your mother, your little sister.

EW: Reconciliation in my memory, yes. But reconciliation meaning physically afterwards? For a while, for many years, I was tempted. I was seduced by them. At one point, I even considered suicide, thinking that they are waiting for me. But I belong to a tradition that believes in life, and, in the eyes of that tradition, whatever is death is impure. Whatever is life is sacred.

BC: Do you expect an explanation, either through revelation here or if there is an afterlife? Do you expect that you might be able to get a full explanation?

EW: Oh, I would like to get it, but I also know I can only get it for myself. That is kind of a Buddhist attitude. The self, the eternal self, the dharma, as the Buddhists call it. For one period in my life I was taken by Buddhism. At that time, I was in India. Whatever I have to find, I know I can find it in the ancient texts. That's why I study Talmud and study the Bible and study Hasidism.[23] I believe in mysticism. I love mystic literature. So whatever is is there.

BC: Does suffering confer moral authority on a person?

EW: Oh, no. Suffering confers no privileges. And, therefore, when people say, "I suffer, therefore . . . " Nonsense. Other people also suffer, and I have no right to measure my suffering against anyone else's suffering. It all depends what I do with that suffering. If I use it to help other people to avoid suffering, then I may have some moral authority, but if I use it in

---

23. **Hasidism** mystical religious movement among Jews

order to increase other people's suffering, then I abuse it, and I have no authority whatsoever.

BC: Please, don't think for a moment that this question is intended to trivialize the most important aspects of your experience, but I think people who admire you would wonder about it. Are there moments of gaiety and spontaneous laughter in your life, or is the enormity of this experience such that it is always with you, that there is a certain solemnity about you at all times?

EW: Oh, no, no. Really not. I laugh, and I am happy, and I love good concerts, and I love my good friends, and we tell jokes to each other. And then I give lectures at the Y, for instance, or at Boston University. I try to introduce as much humor . . . no, I am not a person who believes in macabre[24] or serious despairing moods. Nonsense. I don't have the right to impose that upon anybody else. The opposite: I like good cheer and good theatre and good comedies, and, in general, I think life is not only tears. Life also has happiness to offer and to receive.

BC: Do you worry that as Jewish culture becomes less distinct, at least here in America, and there are pockets of exceptions to that in the Hasidic community, or whatever, but as Jewish culture becomes less distinct and as generational memory blurs as we move further and further from the Holocaust, that the meaning of this will slip further into the ash heap of history, and as witnesses grow older and perish . . .

EW: I do worry. I am not afraid that the event will be forgotten. There were many years in my life that I was afraid that it will be, might be, forgotten. And, therefore, I try to work. I try to inspire and to convince many of my friends also to work. Now I know it won't be forgotten because there are enough documents and books and pictures and even masterworks that will prevent people from forgetting. Today, if I am afraid, and I am afraid, it is that the event will be trivialized, cheapened, reduced to commercial kitsch.[25] That is a source of anguish.

BC: Are all, or almost all, theatrical treatments, movies, stage productions that deal with the Holocaust an affront to you, or can some of them help to illuminate that experience.

EW: Not all, no. Some can. And some do. But the big extravaganzas, I'm afraid, offended many of us.

---

24. **macabre** suggesting the horror of death
25. **kitsch** works considered pretentious and tasteless

BC: Could it ever happen again?

EW: No, I don't think that the Holocaust can ever happen again, meaning the real event, meaning when a state is taken over by a group of fanatics and that group establishes the law, the law of death. But what Germany induced and made other people endure was that it was legal to kill Jews. I don't think it can happen, meaning to establish ghettos and then concentration camps with gas chambers, the whole technique, the technology, the technique of killing, of mass killing, cannot happen. Unless we forget. If we forget, then the forgetting itself would be a tragedy and a crime equal to the tragedy and the crime of those years.

BC: Does it bother you when the word "pogrom"[26] is perhaps misused, trivialized?

EW: Sure.

BC: A recent example (and I am sure that there are many), we have the situation in Crown Heights,[27] where there is undoubtedly a huge strain of anti-Semitism involved and where Jews have been subjected to mistreatment, to hatred and, in a couple of cases, to murder, but it seems to me that even while you decry that, one can certainly make a distinction between that and a pogrom, which . . . has government sanction and is much more systematic than hatred itself.

EW: I agree. I didn't like the word, but then there is a devaluation of many words. A person, let's say, killed eight or nine people, and they call him a mass murderer. Mass murder means something. That doesn't mean that I condone, of course. That is serial murder. It's a good, good word. Why call him mass murderer? Take for example a TV sportscaster speaking about the team that lost, and the commentator said it was a "holocaust" on the field. Now, really. So this kind of devaluation, of cheapening, of reduction—a reductionist attitude—it is, of course, dangerous.

BC: Earlier you spoke of the face of the black sergeant that you saw so vividly when the concentration camp was liberated in April of 1945. And historically, Jews have been on the side of the American civil rights movement.

EW: Oh, yes, yes.

---

26. **pogrom** organized, often officially initiated, persecution and massacre of a minority group, especially of Jews

27. **Crown Heights** section of Brooklyn, New York, where there was tension between African Americans and Hasidic Jews in the early 1990s

BC: How much does it pain you to see the conflict, which is by no means universal (but it exists) between blacks and Jews in New York these days?[28]

EW: It is painful because we are two minorities, and both of them were victimized quite some time. Just today, we had a meeting at the *New York Times* with a group of important people to discuss black and Jewish, to discuss the issue, to see what can be done. Because it is painful, it is scandalous, philosophically scandalous. That shouldn't happen. All kinds of suggestions were made, and, soon, you will hear about them. What to do to bring these two communities together. They must come together.

BC: Do Jews frequently come to you, whether they are Holocaust survivors themselves or they are descendants of Holocaust survivors, and tell you that their faith has failed them?

EW: Yes, very often. Children of survivors, or survivors themselves. But the other way around, too. People come to me saying, "You know, I was not a believer, but then I became a believer." And both are good. If a person comes to me and says, "I used to be a believer, and because of what I saw, I stopped believing," I embrace him. If a person comes and says, "I was not a believer, now I am," I also embrace him. What I don't like is to meet a person who says, "I was a believer before; I am a believer now." It didn't change. Or a disbeliever. That means that if the event had no effect, then something is wrong with that person.

BC: Do the recitations of the events you lived through, such as those you shared with us earlier, do they ever take on a rote quality for you because you've been asked about them in one form or another so many ways? Or are they always vivid in the retelling each time, even if it is five thousand times?

EW: Bob, this is the second time I speak about all that. I don't like to speak about it. In my courses at the university, I don't teach Holocaust literature. When I *was* teaching it, I had to because nobody else did or very few did twenty, twenty-five years ago. But since then, I don't teach. I teach philosophy and literature, Shakespeare and Socrates, and Hasidism, but not Holocaust. And I don't speak about it. And I must confess to you that even today, I thought you were going to speak about *Sages and Dreamers*, about . . .

BC: And we will . . .

---

28. early to mid 1990s

EW: . . . Talmud but not about the Holocaust because I don't like to speak about it. This is the second time. Once I did it, I think, with Bill Moyers, and now with you. So, in all these years, not about the Holocaust, not about my experiences.

BC: And yet you've always said that it's important that you bear witness, that you give some human face to the dimension of this tragedy.

EW: So I have done it with my few books; that means that out of thirty-six books that I have written, I think four or five deal with that subject. And I think it's enough. I'm really too timid. And it's too personal. It costs too much. And I remember I testified at the Barbie[29] trial, although I was not a French victim; I came from Hungary. But all the lawyers and the prosecuting attorneys wrote me a petition I should come and give a kind of general . . . and I remember what it meant to appear there and speak about my little sister. I cannot . . .

BC: At least once in this conversation, but I think only once, you used the word "hatred." No one could blame anybody who was even witness to this, let alone victim of it (and you were both) for hating everybody involved. But hate can consume a person as they move through their life. How have you subdued it or channeled it?

EW: At times I missed it, I wanted it. There were times when I even wrote; I said, we need some kind of hatred. It's normal, it's natural, to channel this hate out, to drive it out, but to *experience* it. Why I didn't— during the war I had other problems on my mind. My father. You know, I really didn't *see* the Germans. I saw the Germans as angels of death. I couldn't lift my eyes. It was forbidden to lift my eyes to see a German SS because he would kill you. After the war, I had my problems: how to readjust, how to readjust to death. It was more difficult to readjust to death than to life, to see in death an exception to the rule, not the normative phenomenon. It was difficult because we were used to death as a normative experience. We lived in death; we lived with death. And then to think about death as a scandal, as a tragedy—it took me some time. So we had to do so many things, really, after the war, to find myself again, and to find the language, to find a life, to find a destiny, to find a family, that I didn't think about that, about hatred. But I knew that it had to exist because it was on the other side. And that's why, since the Nobel Prize, really, I've devoted years to organize seminars all over the world called "Anatomy of Hate." I want to understand the power, the destructive

---

29. **Klaus Barbie** member of the SS, who was arrested in 1983 and convicted of crimes against humanity for his part in World War II

power, of hate. The masks that hate can put on. The language of hate, the technique of hate, the structure of hate, the fabric of hate, the genesis of hate.

BC: Is there a single insight about that that you've come to, that you feel certain of?

EW: I learned from those who participated in a few of my seminars—psychiatrists—saying that a child, until the age of three, doesn't hate. Children can be taught to hate after they are three years old. That means something.

BC: And yet many, many Nazis obviously weren't indoctrinated into Nazi philosophy until they were adults or adolescents. As you said earlier, some moral training, some education, was within them and yet was reversed and perverted.

EW: Hate is an easy temptation, you know. It is seductive. The hater feels superior. The hater not only has power but has the knowledge of the victim. The hater feels like God because he can do with the hated whatever he, or sometimes she, wants. So it's not surprising that so many people in Germany, and in some occupied countries of Eastern Europe, became anti-Semitic and racist and members of xenophobia.[30] They were taken by hatred. It was good for them. I think that ultimately what they will have to learn, if they haven't learned already, is that hate destroys the hater just as it destroys the hated.

BC: Maybe this is silly—it's obvious to me that you are a humble person—but you must sometimes hold in check a certain disdain that you might feel for people who get bogged down in life's trivialities, people who obsess on their own little adversities, when you have seen things on such an enormous scale that you must have a better overview of things than almost anybody else you encounter?

EW: Disdain is a strong word. I do have some disdain for some people.

BC: Impatience . . . "impatience" might have been the word.

EW: Impatience, no . . . I have, rather, amusement. I am amused. I will give you an example. In the beginning, when I began writing, you know, and let's say somebody wrote a nasty review, in the beginning it hurt terribly that these people don't understand, or for some selfish reasons, what they did for jealousy. Silly. And then I said to myself, really, "So what?" You know. "What else can they do to me?" What the Germans hadn't

---

30. **xenophobia** fear of anything strange or foreign

done already. "What else can happen to me?" So I feel amused that they are playing their little games, that's all.

BC: What was the happiest moment of your life?

EW: The birth of my son.

BC: Who carries your father's name.

EW: My father's name. It was something very special, you know. I kept on looking at him, and for years I literally kept on looking at him. Looking and looking. When he was asleep, poor boy—no, I was looking and looking! And even today, I don't want to—I don't like to embarrass him, but I could look at him for hours.

BC: Is there a danger, understandably, where Jews feel such a connection to Israel and to what it represents that sometimes they might overlook—either Jews or supporters of Israel—might overlook the complexities which we can't get into in detail, but it is a complex situation in the Middle East, and there might be a blind adherence to one hundred percent of what are perceived to be Israel's positions?

EW: I can tell you about myself. I love Israel with all my heart. I don't live in Israel, never did. Why I didn't go to Israel after the war is a problem which one day we may try to explore together, but I didn't go. I remained in France first and then came here, but I love Israel with all my heart. That doesn't mean I love Israel's positions. I am not supposed to love or hate Israel's positions. My connection to Israel is based on my traumatized childhood. I have seen what happened to Jews when they were weak, when they were instruments of destiny instead of being the creators of destiny. So when I go to Israel, I feel good. Now it doesn't mean that I don't know what is happening. One of my most heartbreaking moments in my career as a teacher was I came to a university in the Middle West—again, I speak always about literature or philosophy or modern philosophy—and after my lecture a young student got up, and he said, "Professor Wiesel, I don't have a question except the following: I was born in what is now Israel, in Jaffa. And I am an Arab. What do you have to tell me?" And I was so taken by him because there was no hate, no anger, simply a human attempt to make a human contact. What do I say, with my past, with my background as a former refugee, to a young man who is a student who is a refugee? But I answered. I said, "Look, again, let's talk." And we talked, and we talked, and we talked. In one of my books I wrote an open letter to a Palestinian, to a young Palestinian, again, trying to establish contact. I was in Israel. I organized a seminar also on hatred at Haifa University, and one afternoon a group of Palestinians surrounded me with the television on, and they asked me, "How come that you don't speak up for us? You should. We are victims. Why don't you speak up for us?" And I said, "Now, look, if you know me,"—because they said they know what I am doing, my work—I said, "If you know me, you know what I feel about Israel. And I must understand Israel's fears. And I challenge you: help me dispel those fears. And I will speak for you about your hopes and your rights. And you know I don't play games with words." So, therefore, we established a very good contact again. I think Israel is going through, as you said, complex situations, but I have faith in Israel's generosity nevertheless. If Begin,[31] who was a hardliner, could give up the Sinai, he surprised Sadat. Sadat[32] didn't expect him to give up, to give up so much and so easily. I think that when the time comes, and the time will come soon, I'm an optimist.

---

31. **Menachem Begin** prime minister of Israel during negotiations for peace between Israel and Egypt in 1978

32. **Anwar Sadat** Egyptian president in 1978, when Egypt became the first Arab nation to accept the state of Israel

Thane Rosenbaum

Cattle Car Complex

In this short story, the son of Holocaust survivors relives his parents' experiences while he is trapped in an elevator.

HE PUSHED the button marked "Down." He pushed again. The machine ignored the command. Slowly he pivoted his head back, staring up at the stainless-steel eyebrow just over the door. No movement of descending light. The numbers remained frozen, like a row of stalled traffic.

For bodily emphasis, he leaned against the panel—pressing "Down," "Up," "Lobby," "Open," "Close"—trying vainly to breathe some life into the motionless elevator. But there was no pulse. The car remained inert, suspended in the hollow lung of the skyscraper.

"Help!" he yelled. "Get me out of here!" The echo of his own voice returned to him.

Still no transit. The elevator was stuck on 17. A malfunctioning car with a mind for blackjack.

"Remain calm," he reminded himself. "I'll push the emergency alarm."

Then he saw a conspicuous red knob that jutted out more prominently than all the other buttons. Adam reached and pulled. A pulsating ring shook the car and traveled down the shaft, triggering a flood of memories he had buried inside him. He covered his ears; a briefcase dropped to the floor.

"That should reach them," he said, running his hand through his hair, trying to relax.

It was late, well past midnight. Adam Posner had been working on a motion for court the next day. Out his window the lights of the Manhattan skyline glittered with a radiance that belied the stillness of the hour.

A lawyer's life, connected to a punchless carousel of a clock. He hated being among them—being one of them—with their upscale suits and shallow predicaments; these conveniently gymnastic ethical values, bending and mutating with the slightest change of financial weather. Gliding by colleagues in the corridors, walking zombies with glazed eyes and mumbling mouths. No time to exchange pleasantries. That deathly anxiety over deadlines—the exhaust of a tireless treadmill, legs moving fleetingly, furiously.

He played the game reluctantly, knowing what it was doing to his spirit, but also painfully aware of his own legacy, and its contribution to the choices he was destined to make. Above all else he wanted to feel safe, and whatever club offered him the privilege of membership, he was duty-bound to join.

And so another night on the late shift. He was working on behalf of a lucrative client, his ticket to a partnership at the firm. He was the last attorney or staff member to leave that night, something he always sought to avoid. Adam didn't like being alone in dark places, and he didn't like elevators—especially when riding alone.

Some of the lights in the interior hallway had been turned off, leaving a trail of soft shadows along the beige, spotless carpet. His Hermés tie, with the new fleur-de-lis[1] pattern, was hanging from his neck in the shape of a noose, and the two top buttons of his shirt stayed clear of their respective eyelets. A warrior of late-night occupations.

There was a car waiting for him downstairs, one of those plush Lincolns that cater to New York's high-salaried slaves. When he entered the elevator, he could think of nothing but returning to his apartment building, commandeering yet another elevator, and rising to his honeycombed domain overlooking the Empire State Building. He lived alone in a voiceless, sanitized shrine—his very own space in the sky. Not even a pet greeted him, just the hum of an empty refrigerator filled with nothing but a half-empty carton of ice cream, a solitary microwave dinner, and a box of baking soda.

Sleep. How desperately he wanted to sleep. But now the night would take longer to end, and sleep was not yet possible.

"Behave rationally," he said, a lawyerly response to a strained situation. "They'll come and get me. At the very least, they'll need to get the elevator back," he reasoned.

Then with a nervous thumb, he stabbed away at the panel in all manner of chaotic selection. At that moment, any floor, any longitude, would do. Defeated by the inertia of the cab, he ran his hands against the board as though he were playing a harp, palms floating over waves of oval buttons and coded braille, searching for some hidden escape hatch.

The dimensions of the car began to close in on him. The already tight space seemed to be growing smaller, a shrinking enclosure, miniaturizing with each breath.

---

1. **fleur-de-lis** design that looks like a lily

Adam's parents had been in the camps, transported there by rail, cattle cars, in fact. That was a long time ago, another country, another time, another people. An old, trite subject—unfit for dinnertime discussion, not in front of the children, not the way to win friends among Gentiles.[2] The Holocaust fades like a painting exposed to too much sun. A gradual diminishing of interest—once the rallying cry of the modern Diaspora;[3] now like a freak accident of history, locked away in the attic, a hideous Anne Frank, trotted out only occasionally, as metaphorical mirror, reminding those of what was once done under the black eye of indifference.

Adam himself knew a little something about tight, confining spaces. It was unavoidable. The legacy that flowed through his veins. Parental reminiscences had become the genetic material that was to be passed on by survivors to their children. Some family histories are forever silent, transmitting no echoes of discord into the future. Others are like seashells, those curved volutes[4] of the mind—the steady drone of memory always present. All one needs to do is press an ear to the right place. Adam had often heard the screams of his parents at night. Their own terrible visions from a haunted past became his. He had inherited their perceptions of space, and the knowledge of how much one needs to live, to hide, how to breathe where there is no air.

He carried on their ancient sufferings without protest—feeding on the milk of terror; forever acknowledging—with himself as living proof—the umbilical connection between the unmurdered and the long buried.

All his life he had suffered from bouts of claustrophobia, and also a profound fear of the dark. He refused to find his way into a movie theater when the film was already in progress; not even a sympathetic usher could rid him of this paralyzing impasse. At crowded parties he always kept to the door, stationed at the exit, where there was air, where he knew he could get out.

Condemned to living a sleepless nightmare, he began to pace like an animal. His breath grew stronger and more jagged. He tore his glasses from his face and threw them down on the elevator floor. An unbalanced goose step shattered the frames, scattering the pieces around him. Dangling in the air and trapped in a box, a braided copper cable held him hostage to all his arresting fears.

"Where are they? Isn't there someone at the security desk?" He undid yet another shirt button, slamming a fist against the wall. The car rattled with the sound of a screaming saw. He yanked against the strip of a guardrail. It refused to budge. With clenched fists he punched as many num-

---

2. **Gentiles** non-Jewish people
3. **Diaspora** displaced Jews
4. **volutes** turns or whorls

bers of random floors as his stamina allowed, trying to get through to the other side without opening a door. Ramming his head against the panel, he merely encountered the steely panel of unsympathetic buttons. The tantrum finally ended with the thrust of an angry leg.

Adam's chest tightened. A surge of anxiety possessed him. His mind alternated between control and chaos, trying to mediate the sudden emptiness. His eyes lost focus, as though forced to experience a new way of seeing. He wanted to die, but would that be enough? What had once been a reliably sharp and precise lawyer's mind rapidly became undone, replaced by something from another world, from another time, the imprinting of his legacy. Time lost all sensation; each second now palpable and deafening.

"Hel . . . p! Help!"

The sweat poured down his face in sheaths of salt, and the deepening furrows in his forehead assumed a most peculiar epidermal geometry. In abject surrender, with his back against the wall of the car, he slid down to his ankles and covered his face with his hands. Nerves had overtaken his sanity. He was now totally at the mercy of those demons that would deprive him of any rational thought. And he had no one but himself to blame; the psychic pranks of his deepest monstrous self had been summoned, reducing him to a prisoner within the locked walls of the elevator.

Suddenly a voice could be heard, glib scratches filtering through a metallic strainer built right into the panel.

"Hello, hello, are you all right in der, son?"

The voice of God? Adam wondered. So silent at Auschwitz, but here, shockingly, in the elevator—delivered with a surprisingly lilting pitch. An incomprehensible choosing of divine intervention.

"It's the night guard from the lobby. Can ya hear me?"

Adam looked up to the ceiling. He squinted, trying to make out the shapes and sounds of rescue amidst an evolving fog of subconscious turmoil.

"Can ya hear me?" an urgent male voice persisted in reaching him. The voice carried the melody of an Irishman from an outer borough, but Adam, unaccountably, heard only a strident German.

"Yes, I am here," Adam replied, absently, weakly, almost inaudibly.

"Are ya all right?"

"No."

"We 'ave a situation 'ere," the security guard said calmly. "The motor to the elevator is jam'd. I can't repair it from 'ere; so I've called the maint'nance people. There's a fire in another buildin' downtown; and they're busy wit' dat. They said they'll be here as soon as humanly possible. Will you be okay, son?"

Adam lifted himself to his feet, pressed his mouth against the intercom—a static current startled his face—and then screamed: "What do you mean by 'okay'? How can I be okay? This is not life—being trapped in a box made for animals! Is there no dignity for man?" After another pause, he wailed, "You are barbarians! Get me out!"

The guard's lips pursed with all due bewilderment, and his tone sank. "You 'aven't been inside der long, mister. I know ya want to get out and go home for de night, but let's not make this a bigger ordeal than it already 'tis."

Adam then volunteered the nature of this "ordeal."

"Why should we be forced to resettle? This is our home. We are Germans! We have done nothing wrong! Nazis! Murderers! Nazis!"

The lobby of the building was barren, the only sound the quiet gurgle of water dripping down the side of a Henry Moore fountain. The stark marble walls were spare. The interior lights dimmed for the evening.

The security guard pondered Adam's reply, and then muttered to himself: "It takes all kinds. The elevator gets stuck, and he calls me a Nazi. Who told him to labor so long? . . ." Recovering, he picked up the receiver and said, "I'm sorry, sir. I don't get your meanin'. Say, ya got a German in der wit' ya?"

"We can't breathe in here! And the children, what will they eat? How can we dispose of our waste? We are not animals! We are not cattle! There are no windows in here, and the air is too thin for all of us to share. You have already taken our homes. What more do you want? Please give us some air to breathe."

By now the guard was joined by the driver of the limousine, who had been parked on Third Avenue waiting for Adam to arrive. The driver, a Russian émigré, had grown anxious and bored, staring out onto an endless stream of yellow cabs; honking fireflies passing into the night, heading up-town. By radio he called his dispatcher, trying to find out what had happened to his passenger, this Mr. Posner, this lawyer who needed the comforts of a plush sedan to travel thirty blocks back to his co-op. The dispatcher knew of no cancellation. Adam Posner was still expected downstairs to claim his ride. This was America after all, the driver mused. The elite take their time and leave others waiting.

So the driver left his car to stretch his legs. Electronically activated doors opened as he entered the building and shuffled over a burnished floor to a circular reception pedestal. The security guard was still struggling to communicate with Adam.

"I am looking for a Mr. Posner," the driver said, with Russian conviction. "I should pick him up outside, and to drive him to Twenty-ninth Street, East Side. Do you know this man?"

With a phone cradled under his chin, and a disturbed expression on his face, the guard said, "All I know is we have an elevator down, and at least one man stuck inside. But who knows who—or what—else he's got in der with 'im. I tink he's actin' out parts in a play. To tell you the truth, he sounds a bit daft to me."

With the aplomb[5] of a police hostage negotiator, the Russian said, "Let me talk to him. I'll find out who he is." The guard shrugged as the phone changed hands. The Russian removed his angular chauffeur's cap and wiped his brow. A determined expression seized his face as he lifted the cradle to his mouth, and said, "Excuse me. Is a Mr. Posner in there?"

"What will become of the women and children?" Adam replied. "Why should we be resettled in Poland?" He did not wait for a reply. A brief interlude of silence was then followed by a chorus of moans and shrieks, as if a ward in a veterans' hospital had become an orchestra of human misery, tuning up for a concert. "I don't believe they are work camps! We won't be happy. We will die there! I can feel it!"

The Russian was himself a Jew and winced with all too much recognition. "Is this Mr. Posner?" he continued. "This is your limo. Don't worry, we will get you out. We will rescue you."

Adam now heard this man from Brighton Beach with his Russian accent, the intoned voice of liberation. Who better to free him from his bondage than a Bolshevik from the east—in this case from Minsk or Lvov—the army that could still defeat the Germans. "Liberate us! We are starving! We are skeletons, walking bones, ghosts! Get us out of this hell!"

"What's 'e sayin'?" the security guard asked.

"I'm not exactly sure, but I think it has something to do with the Holocaust, my friend."

"Ah, de Holycost; a terrible thing, dat."

The Russian nodded—the recognition of evil, a common language between them. "I'll talk to him again," he said, and grabbed the intercom again. "Mr. Posner, don't worry. We will get you out. You are not in camps. You are not in cattle car. You are just inside elevator, in your office building. You are a lawyer; you've worked late. You are tired, and scared. You must calm down."

"Calm down, calm down, so easy for you Russians to say," Adam replied abruptly. "We have been selected for extermination. We cannot survive. Who will believe what has happened to us? Who will be able to comprehend? Who will say kaddish[6] for me?"

The lobby was crowding up. Two drowsy-looking repairmen, their sleep disturbed by the downtown fire and now this, entered the building and went up to the guard console. "What's the problem here?" one of them asked. "We're with the elevator company."

Fully exasperated, the guard indignantly replied, "Ya want to know what's wrong, do ya? Ya want to know what the *problem* is? I'll tell ya! It's supposed to be de graveyard shift. Piece o' cake, they say, nothin' ever hap-

---

5. **aplomb** poise
6. **kaddish** Jewish prayer

pens, right? Not when I'm on duty. No, sir. When I'm 'ere, graveyard means all the ghosts come out, the mummies, the wackos! We 'ave a loony tune stuck in one o' the elevators!" Jauntily, winking at one of the maintenance men, he added, "I think de guy in de elevator thinks he's in some . . . World War Two movie."

"This man in elevator is not crazy," the Russian driver said in defense. "It is world that is crazy; he is only one of its victims. Who knows what made him like this?"

One of the repairmen dashed off to the control room. Moments later he returned, carrying a large mechanical device, an extraction that would bring the night to an end and allow everyone to go home. "I think I fixed the problem," he announced. "It was just a jammed crank."

As he was about to finish explaining the exploits behind the repair, the elevator began its appointment with gravity. The four men moved from the center of the lobby and gathered in front of the arriving elevator car.

"Should we ring an ambulance?" the security guard wondered. "I hope I don't lose me wages over this. I've done all anyone could. You know," he gestured toward the limousine driver, "you were here." The driver refused to take his eyes off the blinking lights, the overhead constellation that signaled the car's gradual descent.

The elevator glided to a safe stop. Like a performer on opening night, the car indulged in a brief hesitation—a momentary hiccup, of sorts—before the doors opened.

As the elevator doors separated like a curtain, the four men, in one tiny choreographed step, edged closer to the threshold, eager to glimpse the man inside. Suddenly there was a collective shudder, and then a retreat.

The unveiling of Adam Posner.

Light filtered into the car. The stench of amassed filth was evident. It had been a long journey. An unfathomable end.

Adam was sitting on the floor, dressed in soiled rags. Silvery flecks of stubble dappled his bearded face. Haltingly, he stared at those who greeted him. Were they liberators or tormentors? He did not yet know. His eyes slowly adjusted to the light, as though his confinement offered nothing but darkness. He presented the men of the transport with an empty stare, a vacancy of inner peace. As he lifted himself to his feet, he reached for a suitcase stuffed with a life's worth of possessions, held together by leather straps fastened like rope. Grabbing his hat and pressing it on his head, Adam emerged, each step the punctuation of an uncertain sentence. His eyes were wide open as he awaited the pronouncement: right or left, in which line was he required to stand?

Bob Keeler

Assault on History

In 1994, reporter Bob Keeler examined the small group of people who believe that the Holocaust never happened. This group of self-proclaimed Holocaust revisionists attempts to spread its message by buying ads in college newspapers.

FOR THE small but increasingly visible group of people who deny history by spreading the perverse claim that the Holocaust is little more than a long-running Jewish hoax, these are interesting times.

Though the Steven Spielberg film *Schindler's List* has dramatically heightened awareness of the Holocaust and reinforced the cold historical truth of Nazi genocide, it has not slowed the movement of Holocaust-denial, spread in the past three years mainly through advertisements in college newspapers by a small band of California-based propagandists. The ad campaign has led to media coverage of denial doctrine and significantly elevated the profile of the self-proclaimed Holocaust "revisionists."

One of their ads appeared in this week's issue of the independent student newspaper at Queens College, the latest instance of the deniers causing a campus commotion with an ad challenging the United States Holocaust Memorial Museum to prove that the Nazis gassed Jews to death during World War II.

There is, of course, no real debate about the Nazis' "Final Solution." The documented truth is that Hitler's Germany mounted a systematic program for the destruction of European Jewry and killed as many as 6 million Jews and millions of others. In 1991, confronted by deniers at its meeting in Chicago, the American Historical Association voted unanimously to condemn Holocaust denial, saying: "No serious historian questions that the Holocaust took place." When a group of deniers showed up at a meeting last month in San Francisco, the association's governing council reaffirmed that statement.

Still, American scholars and Jewish leaders say they worry that the deniers, who almost universally lack any scholarly credentials, have made progress in spreading their grotesque gospel—essentially, that Jews used the Holocaust "hoax" to steal reparations from Germany and to justify the creation of Israel on Arab lands. Over the years, deniers have also claimed that concentration-camp crematoria were used to dispose of those who died of natural causes and did not have a large enough capacity to produce 6 million deaths; that only a few hundred thousand Jews died, most of them from disease; even that *The Diary of Anne Frank* was a fraud.

Such outlandish claims go back 25 years in this country, and to immediately after World War II in Argentina and parts of Europe. But now, American Jewish leaders say they are concerned that the deniers might be finding a receptive audience in this country, with polls showing significant numbers of Americans ignorant about the Holocaust. In one finding, by the Roper Organization for the American Jewish Committee in 1992, 22 percent of adults and 20 percent of high school students answered that "it seems possible that the Nazi extermination of the Jews never happened." Another 12 percent of adults and 17 percent of students said they didn't know.

"One of the things they have achieved is that they have put their propositions on the public agenda," said Jeffrey Ross of the Anti-Defamation League of B'nai B'rith.[1] To Ross and others, the deniers play on ignorance and bigotry to advance their real agenda.

"The bottom line is anti-Semitism," said Marvin Stern, Pacific Northwest regional director of the Anti-Defamation League. "You can't intellectually combat Holocaust denial." As a result, Holocaust scholars and Jewish leaders say, their problem is one of strategy: how to combat the deniers without dignifying them—and being drawn into a debate about the undebatable. "It's the historical equivalent of two plus two equals five," said Deborah Lipstadt, a professor of Jewish studies at Emory University in Atlanta and author of the recent book *Denying the Holocaust: The Growing Assault on Truth and Memory*.

A rise in Holocaust awareness over the past year may help, Jewish leaders say. Since its opening nine months ago in Washington, the United States Holocaust Memorial Museum has drawn 1.4 million visitors and generated a flood of publicity. And *Schindler's List*, which has earned 12 Academy Award nominations, is already the most commercially successful film treatment of the Holocaust. It has been playing to sold-out theaters since its release in December. The museum clearly vexes[2] the deniers, who are attacking it in their ads. But like other films and books about the Holocaust, *Schindler's List* leaves the deniers unmoved.

---

1. **B'nai B'rith** Jewish service organization
2. **vexes** angers

"They may see Spielberg's movie as something that they don't like, because it hits home in graphic terms," says Kenneth Stern, author of a 1993 American Jewish Committee book on Holocaust denial. "On the other hand, they will probably dismiss it as just another 'exterminationist' point of view."

That's exactly what the deniers say. "It's just part of the ongoing and seemingly never-ending Holocaust campaign, which is supported not only by Hollywood, but by our government," said Mark Weber, editor of the *Journal of Historical Review,* which attempts to give deniers credibility by looking like a respected scholarly journal.

"The problem here is that there is so little evidence," said Ted O'Keefe, who is reviewing *Schindler's List* for the May/June issue of the publication, which is put out by the academic-sounding Institute for Historical Review but deals almost exclusively with Holocaust denial. The 15-year-old organization, based in Newport Beach, Calif., claims a mailing list of 30,000 and a budget of $500,000, mostly from sales of books and tapes challenging the Holocaust.

O'Keefe's claims are typical of the deniers' dogma.[3] "Except for the cartoonish figures of the Nazis and the explicit brutality, the film in terms of establishing the Holocaust is essentially an argument by innuendo," said O'Keefe, one of seven full-time staff members of the Institute for Historical Review. In fact, the deniers say there is nothing unusual about the film's portrayal of Jews surviving. They have argued that there were more Jews after the war than before. In any event, said O'Keefe, "We tend to welcome these cultural explosions, because they tend to keep the spotlight on us."

Though historians reject all the deniers' claims as anti-Semitic nonsense, some Jewish leaders feel the need to keep the evidence coming. With the fall of the Soviet Union, they expect millions of pages of Nazi documents to become available, allowing scholars in the next few years to fill in the remaining gaps in information about what happened to Jews in the areas of Europe controlled by the Soviets after World War II.

"We believe that good scholarship ultimately drives fraud from the marketplace," said Michael Berenbaum, director of the United States Holocaust Research Institute in Washington, whose book, *Anatomy of the Death Camp Auschwitz,* will be published this spring by Indiana University Press.

The deniers dismiss not only the work of serious researchers, but the testimony of Holocaust survivors. For these survivors, the denial of their fearsome suffering is a source of great pain.

One such survivor is Edith Vardy of Great Neck. When a friend told her about a radio discussion of Holocaust deniers, Vardy was unprepared. "I was shocked," she said. "It was so hurting me, the whole thing."

---

3. **dogma** belief

Vardy's mother and two small brothers went through the Auschwitz gas chambers on May 20, 1944, the day the family arrived from a ghetto in Hungary. For the next eight months, the young Edith Heimann and her sister, Elish-ewa, lived in a barracks separated by an electrified fence from a gas chamber and crematorium. Their job was to tear apart the personal effects of those killed in the gas chamber and look for valuables. They divided the possessions into piles, and she remembers one was a heartbreaking hill of infant pacifiers.

In those eight months Vardy saw how the Nazis lulled the gas chamber victims by telling them to hang their clothes up carefully and remember where they had put them, as if they were coming back. She heard prisoners screaming inside the chambers. She learned how the Nazis forced Jewish prisoners to run the gas chamber and crematoria, then killed them and used new prisoners.

The evening before one of those groups was to die, she remembers, a Hungarian doctor told her that he and other prisoners had agreed to sign a document attesting they had "operated the crematoria only for people who died naturally."

A reporter related Vardy's experience to Bradley Smith, the man behind the college newspaper ads. He calls his group the Committee for Open Debate on the Holocaust. Smith was unmoved. "There were no gas chambers there," Smith said. "This stuff is just junk."

The insouciant[4] rejection of evidence and the whole denial enterprise, Jewish leaders argue, has a simple goal: to make the racist, ethnocentric[5] agenda of neofascism[6] more acceptable by casting doubt on the unspeakable crimes of the Nazis, which gave fascism an intolerable odor.

The roots of denial lie in the rise of neofascist groups in Europe in the 1960s and 1970s, says Emory's Deborah Lipstadt. The deniers got a shot in the arm in 1976 with the publication of a book called *The Hoax of the Twentieth Century*, by a Northwestern University electrical engineering professor named Arthur Butz. His book was a breakthrough: Published by a small outfit known for racist and anti-Semitic literature, it was nonetheless the first appearance of Holocaust-denial claims outside the neo-Nazi fringe, in a work festooned with all the trappings of scholarship, such as bibliography and footnotes.

The Butz book remains a top seller for the Institute for Historical Review, which was founded in 1978 and is now at the heart of the deniers' world. One of its founders was Willis Carto, also the founder of the Liberty Lobby, which the conservative columnist William Buckley called "a hotbed

---

4. **insouciant** casual or carefree
5. **ethnocentric** based on attitude that one's own group is superior
6. **fascism** dictatorship or extreme nationalism

of anti-Semitism." Carto is described by Kenneth Stern of the American Jewish Committee as "one of the most energetic, long-standing professional anti-Semites in the United States today." (Carto did not return a call to the Liberty Lobby in Washington).

The number of true disbelievers today, and whether it is growing, is unclear. "The numbers are probably small, but when you have a hating group like that, you don't need large numbers," Lipstadt said. The paid circulation of the *Journal of Historical Review* has tripled in the last year, to 6,000, claims Mark Weber, the editor. He said the institute's conferences, which are held every year or two, attract 150 to 200 people.

In combating what they see as the deniers' growing visibility, historians say they are hard-pressed to deal with them responsibly. "This has been a difficult project, because at times I have felt compelled to prove something I knew to be true," Lipstadt wrote in her book. "I had constantly to avoid being inadvertently sucked into a debate that is no debate and an argument that is no argument."

In fact, a California court has taken "judicial notice" of the Holocaust—a legal term that means stipulating an obvious fact about which there is no debate. The case arose from a 1979 challenge by the Institute for Historical Review, offering $50,000 to anyone who "could prove that the Nazis operated gas chambers to execute Jews during World War II." The offer was designed to get publicity for the institute, then only a year old. The publicity came, but at a high cost.

In its bulletin, the institute carried an open letter to one Auschwitz survivor, Mel Mermelstein, a California shipping-pallet manufacturer who had criticized the institute in letters to newspapers. The institute accused Mermelstein of "peddling the extermination hoax" and challenged him to provide proof. Mermelstein, the only survivor from a family of six, responded with a notarized description of his own experience, among other information. When the institute rejected his submission, Mermelstein sued.

In 1981, Los Angeles County Superior Court Judge Thomas Johnson ruled that the Holocaust was "not reasonably subject to dispute," adding: "The court does take judicial notice that Jews were gassed to death in Poland in Auschwitz in the summer of 1944," when Mermelstein and his family were there.

"In 1985, I won a stipulated judgment for $150,000, which I decided to reduce to $90,000, provided they pay in a certain way: I wanted to get paid forthwith," Mermelstein said. The institute sent him checks for $50,000 and $20,000 on time, but the final $20,000 check was delayed in the mail. Mermelstein took them back to court over that, determined not to give the deniers even an inch of slack. "I got the full $90,000, plus $38.36 for late payment," he said. In 1990, his story became a television movie starring Leonard Nimoy.

The Mermelstein case hardly fazed the deniers. "These guys are working for the long run," said Ross, of the Anti-Defamation League. "They know full well that ten or fifteen years down the road, there is going to be no one left who's a survivor." In her book, Lipstadt said that they aim to "plant seeds of doubt that will bear fruit in coming years . . ."

At least in America, there may be some fertile soil for those seeds of doubt. In the 1992 Roper survey, 38 percent of adults and 53 percent of high school students could not say what the term "Holocaust" refers to. The study also found that the significant percentage of Americans that believes it's possible Nazi genocide didn't happen cuts through lines of age, education and background. In Britain and France, polls turned up much lower receptivity to Holocaust denial. A poll is now under way in Germany.

Berenbaum, the Holocaust researcher, says some of the willingness to question history may be attributable to an American kind of cynicism about anything official. And some people, he said, may be unwilling to believe something so barbaric could actually happen in the modern world.

"The real issue here is ignorance," said David Singer, the American Jewish Committee's polling expert. While there is no evidence that deniers created these attitudes, Singer said, they might be able to exploit them. The organization plans to conduct a new survey next month to assess whether the Holocaust museum and *Schindler's List* have had any effect.

The deniers have two other things working for them: the aura of respectability they have cultivated and the American devotion to free speech. Though Jewish leaders insist that deniers are motivated by anti-Semitism, deniers don't always look or sound the part. "When you meet them, they're not frothing at the mouth, and they're not yelling, 'Heil Hitler,'" Lipstadt said.

Demonstrating a concern for public relations, the Institute for Historical Review recently bounced Willis Carto, apparently because he was pushing positions that might damage its scholarly image. "Carto over the last couple of years became interested in turning the IHR from its revisionist, scholarly course," O'Keefe said. "It would have involved lowering our editorial standards, and it would have involved bringing in stuff on race and other polemical issues that we wanted to stay clear of."

In the long term, the biggest public relations problem for the deniers may turn out to be *Schindler's List*, already acclaimed as the greatest feature film ever made about the Holocaust. But while Marvin Stern said it may help fill "that vacuum of knowledge in the popular culture," Lipstadt cautioned: "There is no finality to anti-Semitism and prejudice."

For the dwindling number of Holocaust survivors, the deniers have given them an enhanced sense of duty to tell their stories. "I don't have a right not to," Edith Vardy said.

When she dies, Vardy told her son Michael, she wants the arm with the Auschwitz tattoo removed and left for a museum. "This should be for the next generation, for the deniers," she said, holding out her arm. "I will not talk from my grave, but my hand should be here."

Rewriting History 101:

Bob Keeler

Bradley Smith's Campus Campaign

WHEN THE ad from Bradley Smith's Committee for Open Debate on the Holocaust arrived on the campus of Brandeis University, the editorial board of the college paper, *The Justice*, voted overwhelmingly to publish it. "I believe, as a journalist, as a human and as a Jew, that this advertisement needs to be published to expose anti-Semitism for what it is," said Howard Jeruchimowitz, a member of the board who has since become the paper's editor.

Getting the ad—promoting the idea the Nazis never operated gas chambers—published on a campus where two-thirds of the students are Jewish was Smith's "greatest achievement," said Jeffrey Ross, director of campus affairs and higher education for the Anti-Defamation League of B'nai B'rith, and one of Smith's most vocal opponents.

On campus, however, the decision was not so popular. The paper's editor was threatened, and his car was vandalized. Two-thousand copies of the newspaper disappeared. And while the Brandeis editors say they made a reasoned judgment with the best of intentions, Holocaust scholars say it was a typical response by Smith's young targets.

Holocaust experts who closely monitor and condemn the acceptance of the ads say that Smith, a former concrete contractor and now full-time Holocaust denier, preys on the idealism and naivete[1] of college students. They say that some don't seem to understand that the First Amendment does not require a college paper—or any paper—to print anything. "What he's doing is using the First Amendment not as a shield but as a sword," Ross said last week at a seminar on deniers at Queens College. The meeting was prompted by controversy over the acceptance of Smith's ad by the college paper, *The Quad*. About 30 percent of the students at Queens are Jewish.

Smith's California-based advertising campaign is the front line of the Holocaust-denial war. In the three years that Smith has been sending his ads to college newspapers (which have inexpensive advertising and can offer chances

---

1. **naivete** innocence or gullibility

for controversy and publicity), more than 30 papers have accepted them, including daily college newspapers at major campuses such as Northwestern, Duke, Cornell and Ohio State universities and the University of Michigan.

Protests have followed some decisions to accept the ad. The student editors of the Ohio State *Lantern*, one of the largest college dailies, triggered a campus uproar when they decided to publish the ad. "It is repulsive to think that the quality, or the total lack thereof, of any idea or opinion has any bearing on whether it should be heard," the editors explained in an editorial. At other campuses, editors have printed the ad to "expose" Smith and the deniers.

Some student editors have tried to take the sting out of running the ad by giving the money to charity. Andrew Wallenstein, editor of *The Quad* at Queens College, which deleted Smith's address and solicitation of funds, said he would return Smith's $230 dollar check. "So then he's giving Bradley Smith free space," complained Michael Berenbaum, director of the United States Holocaust Research Institute.

The Quad ran the ad on its front page, next to an editorial describing it as a "sham" that was the moral equivalent of a swastika. Inside, the paper ran a full-page letter from college President Shirley Strum Kenny criticizing the acceptance of the ad.

Last fall, Smith managed to get the ad into a general-circulation newspaper, *The Portland Oregonian*. The ad "was repugnant and we regret having published it," the *Oregonian* said later. "It fell through the cracks," said the publisher, Fred Stickel.

Smith, 63, who grew up in South Central Los Angeles, became a Holocaust "revisionist" after reading one of the main denial books, *The Hoax of the Twentieth Century*, by Arthur Butz. In 1987 he founded the Committee for Open Debate on the Holocaust with Mark Weber, the editor of the *Journal of Historical Review*. The committee now consists of Smith and five regional directors.

Smith says he concentrates on about 200 colleges. His current ad, the fourth in the series, challenges the United States Holocaust Museum to prove that the Nazis gassed even one Jew to death. Smith continues circulating the ad, but at Brandeis, for one, it is now history. "I'm more interested in how the Jewish community is going to deal with Bradley R. Smith, neo-Nazis and anti-Semitism," Jeruchimowitz said. "Personally, I'd like to take his stuff and throw it out."

The Captives' Hymn

Helen Colijn

In this true story, Helen Colijn recalls how women found the strength and courage to survive a Japanese internment camp during World War II.

OUR CAMP was the responsibility of a succession of Japanese officers in well-pressed uniforms and tall polished boots. We often did not see our camp commander for weeks. He probably hates the sight of us, we figured, the reason for his being stuck on this dull outpost on Sumatra, far from the glory of military action.

The Japanese we did see and have to deal with daily were generally uneducated, uncouth,[1] unkempt[2] common soldiers. They were the men who counted us, ignored all of our requests, and occasionally treated us to their vile tempers.

The guards were particularly nasty when filled with rice wine. Then they would explode into a rage because a woman had the audacity[3] to take a crate off the food truck to be used as a seat. Or because she was not properly dressed in anticipation of an officer's camp inspection. (Of course, she could only appear wearing the skimpy camp uniform of shorts and suntop because the plea for material had been ignored.) Or the guards would tear through one of the houses, ripping mattress pads, emptying suitcases and storage bags, in search of forbidden diaries.

But one day a guard strolled over to a house where some Australian women were entertaining and made signs at the window that he wanted to

---

1. **uncouth** rude or uncivilized
2. **unkempt** messy
3. **audacity** courage or boldness

be invited in. No one in the house wanted him inside. He was offered a seat on the dustbin,[4] raised for his benefit to window-level, and from there he watched the women. He was thoroughly amused and laughed hard at a pantomime[5] two women put on.

Another guard asked the same women (in July) to sing "Auld Lang Syne" for him. They did, and he politely said "*Arigato*," Japanese for "thank you."

But always, just when we began thinking that the Japanese might not be so bad after all, an awful thing would happen.

Behind the Australians' house the usual "black market" exchange was going on. A Chinese fellow was caught in the act of throwing a loaf of bread over the barbed-wire fence. The guards dragged him into the camp and tied him to a pole. They raised his arms above his head and tied a rope to his hands and neck in such a way that it would strangle him when he lowered his arms.

Mother Laurentia begged the guards to take him away, to no avail. We were not to help him in any way. One of the English boys defied the order and gave the man some water. During the night, someone put a knotted handkerchief over the man's head. The next morning, when the guard saw it, he yanked it off. It took three days for the man to die. This cruel spectacle was particularly hard on the children, who had to walk by the man on the way to *tenko*.[6]

We had barely recovered from this shocking event when the mothers were told to send their eleven- and twelve-year-old sons to the guardhouse. The nine boys cast worried glances backward as they trooped away. Their fearful mothers wondered if their sons would return.

They did. But only briefly. "We have to be ready at four o'clock. We are being sent to a men's camp."

Pandemonium. "Which camp? Where?"

"We do not know."

One of the boys, Theo Rottier, recently related what happened:

"We had to walk through a corridor into a backyard, a walled backyard—a perfect scene for an execution. They ordered us to undress. One of the boys whispered, 'Hey, we're not going to do that!' The Japanese overheard him. After a few slaps and a few kicks, we were out of our pants in no time. And there we stood, naked, and they looked at us. They said, 'You, you, you . . . report at four o'clock with your personal belongings."

In vain, the mothers argued that their sons were still children and better off with their mothers. The Japanese retorted, "They are now men! They will go to a men's camp!"

---

4. **dustbin** garbage can
5. **pantomime** story told by means of gesture and facial expression
6. **tenko** roll-call

The boys marched behind the guard out of the camp, trying to hide their fear. They had no idea where they were going. The mothers put up a brave front, too. But after the boys were gone, they cried.

It was many weeks before we heard that the boys had been sent to our men in the Palembang jail. Some boys found their fathers there; some knew no one at all, and were assigned a camp "uncle."

Throughout our internment, the Japanese remained impossible to fathom or understand. Even Tine, who had lived in Japan, admitted she couldn't "read" them.

I have since wondered whether a mediator fluent in Japanese and knowledgeable about our very different cultures could have improved the women's lot by creating mutual understanding. As it was, we thought the Japanese were totally alien creatures, and we must have seemed equally alien to them. What a change we were from the stereotypical Japanese woman, so submissive, obedient, and patient. We argued with the guards and complained endlessly. In the Japanese culture, I later learned, complaining about discomfort is bad manners.

In the years before the war the Japanese had been firmly indoctrinated[7] with the idea that the Japanese spirit can conquer anything—fatigue, hunger, and enemy cannons. And here were we whites, who had lost the war, and we had the bad manners to make extravagant demands for furniture and food. Why, the Japanese themselves didn't have many comforts in their homeland. We must have matched perfectly their notion of luxury-oriented Westerners, making a big noise whenever they were displeased.

I don't think that many of us were aware—I certainly wasn't—of how inferior we must have appeared to the Japanese for these reasons. Besides, we had let ourselves be taken prisoner. The Japanese had nothing but contempt for soldiers who let themselves be captured. In the past such men returning to Japan had actually been executed or ostracized from the community. Suicide was often their only honorable way out. We women were not soldiers, and had nothing to do with the warfare, but . . . we were still women, low on the Japanese social totem pole.

One day, a guard drove a truck into the camp, looking very pleased with himself. He brought us a heavy, six-foot wooden pole for a "pestle" and a round block, two feet across and hollowed out, for a "mortar."

"This is to make your life easier," he managed to communicate to the bystanders. We would have to heave the pole up and down to pound rice, as I had seen women do in villages on Java. I had even taken pictures of them. So picturesque, those women in colorful sarongs[8] and tight-fitting tops,

---

7. **indoctrinated** educated
8. **sarongs** skirtlike outer garments

often working in pairs and chanting as they raised and lowered the pole with unvarying rhythm, up and down . . . Of us three, Antoinette became the best pounder, with her characteristic persistence.

The block was stationed at the end of Irenelaan. I had gone up to watch Antoinette, who was pounding our ration of hard, dollar-sized slices of dried cassava[9] called *gaplék*. Her brief black shorts, cut down from the pedal pushers she had received after the shipwreck, her little red-checkered suntop made from a dishtowel, and her bare arms, legs, and feet were already velvety from the dust of the flour.

"Why don't you stop? You can't pulverize those nasty little bits," I suggested.

"I'm sure I can get more flour yet. Besides, pounding helps me get rid of frustration. Think of it, already six months in this camp . . ." and she went on pounding faster and harder.

Finally she gave up, and with an empty Quaker Oats tin scooped the flour and residue out of the block onto a borrowed winnow[10] about as large as a bicycle wheel. Holding the winnow with both hands, she shook it, until a hillock[11] of flour lay on one side of the winnow and the residue on the other. Then she slid the flour into the tin and tossed the residue at the side of the street. "Tonight it's *ongel-ongel* for dinner, Helen." Ongel-ongel was the name we used for a porridge made of this flour and water. It had a slimy, glue-like consistency and tasted as awful as it sounded.

"No, you won't have to eat ongel-ongel," said Alette, who had just joined Antoinette and me at the block. "I made some bread."

Bread in the camp was a concoction cooked in a double boiler made from a Quaker Oats tin and a powdered milk tin. "I used the rice flour I pounded for us a few days ago."

"How is Baby Wim today?" I asked. Alette was carrying him in her arms.

"He's getting heavy, already four months old."

Wim Wenning was one of six babies born in the camp. His mother was an artist, and she did not mother well. Alette was passing through house number 13 one day and noticed that he had a dirty diaper. He was alone, his mother nowhere in sight. Alette located her, received a clean diaper, changed the baby, and washed the dirty diaper. The mother was delighted. Before long Alette did all the baby's laundry, fed him, and often entertained him when his mother was off working on her art projects.

I had been surprised to see this side of Alette. But then, I did not really know her well because of separations in our family. For example, for three

---

9. **cassava** nutritious starch made from the roots of a cassava plant

10. **winnow** pan

11. **hillock** small mound

years she lived with Father and Mother in an outpost on Borneo, Mother teaching her the first three years of grade school with a correspondence course, while Antoinette and I lived with a Dutch family in The Hague and went to schools there. As I discussed this maternal side of "our little sister" with Antoinette, she recalled how Alette took care of her pets on Borneo. Mother sent us photos of Alette feeding ducks, miniature deer or exotic birds or pushing Beppo in a stroller. Beppo was a baby orangutan. He had been found in the jungle after a hunter had shot his mother. When Mother took Alette back to Holland, Beppo was shipped to a zoo in The Hague. A spacious cage awaited him, where Alette would go and visit. The still small orangutan with the mahogany-colored hair and the girl with the blond locks hugged each other while zoo visitors outside the cage "oohed" and "aahed."

I asked Alette one day in the camp why she spent so much time on someone else's baby. She answered, "He's cute. And when I can help his mother, she can spend more time on the camp newspaper. That way, I indirectly contribute to the newspaper."

There was an English and a Dutch edition, typed with carbon copies on the camp's rickety typewriter and issued to each house. I still have a copy of the introductory issue, dated August 16, 1942. The masthead[12] showed that the staff of six was equally divided between the "English" and the Dutch. The opening editorial read:

> We have the pleasure in starting a new periodical on its career and trust it will receive a welcome. Although we are not a large community, it is surprising how little we know about each other, and we hope that by sharing a common news bulletin we may help to strengthen the bonds between us by getting to know each other. "United we stand, divided we fall" is a saying that has proved true only too frequently of late. We trust that we shall learn to weld ourselves into a common loyalty and aim, sharing each other's joys and troubles and working for a common purpose . . . So this little paper joins the ranks of the newly born in the camp. May its career be successful, though none of us wishes it will be long.

"Church Notices" mentioned services in English and Dutch, Sunday schools, Bible studies. "Medical Notices" urged the pounding of egg shells (if we ever got an egg again) to create calcium powder for daily intake. This column warned, "There are many tropical sores in the camp. These are caused by dirty flies and mosquitoes which settle on every small scratch of the body. The flies and mosquitoes live on garbage and in the open drains

---

12. **masthead** notice in newspaper or magazine that gives the title, staff, publisher's name and other information

[that ran before the houses] and cause infection: do cover the smallest scratch."

Rita Wenning had designed a camp emblem that was shown in the paper. "It is representing the British and The Netherlands flags. The cross formed between the flagstaffs symbolizes the cross we have to bear in common. The sparkling diamond in the intersection represents the noble effort of the internees of both nationalities to beautify their lives."

And beautify our lives we did in various ways. Some of the "English" instituted the ritual of morning "elevenses" (snack or beverage at eleven o'-clock) and afternoon tea. Each *kongsi* member washed her hands, if there was water in the tap, combed her hair with the kongsi comb, and sat around a table of sorts. This was probably a crate or a plank on a suitcase, decorated with a flower if a bush near the barbed wire was in bloom.

The "tea" was a brew made from roasted rice. Invitees sipped genteelly[13] from the half-coconut shells or chipped cups brought from home. Sometimes "cookies" were served—tiny rice patties baked on a tin. Spoons to stir the brew varied from a real silver spoon missed by the looters to a shoe horn; most resembled the little spoons used nowadays in Chinese restaurants. It was a hallowed rule that conversation on these occasions was not to be about the camp. Guests were often asked to tell a joke, recite a poem, or play a famous person in a game of charades.

At one of the tea charades, I arrived mimicking sleep by putting both hands together against an ear, cocking my head, closing my eyes. I had fastened a piece of paper with a letter "O" to my sun halter and stuck a long thin tail, its bushy end made from material scraps, to my shorts. I was Nap-O-Leon, and everyone guessed it.

In the camp I thought those make-believe teas silly. Now I realize that the structure and etiquette those meetings imposed helped to make an untenable living situation more tenable.

"Cultural" events took place. We already had our singing groups. Now lectures were presented out on Irenelaan at night. During the day it was too hot and the asphalt would stick to our bare feet—or to our behinds if we sat down. At night, a full or near-full moon would provide light to see by. The electric street lamps that had shined so brightly when we arrived had long remained dark because of the black-out.

Lecture subjects included butterfly collecting, astronomy, rubber harvesting, and whatever else anyone felt knowledgeable enough to talk about.

Lessons were popular among adults. Shelagh's mother taught beginning English to some of the Dutch, writing a primer with little pictures. Antoinette did Mensendieck exercises with any woman willing to get hot

---

13. **genteelly** politely

and sweaty doing knee bends and working her abdominal muscles.

I gave Dutch lessons to Australian nurses. The lessons were punctuated by roars of laughter as the girls attempted to pronounce the Dutch "g," and were discontinued when the group needed time to work on a mah-jongg set.[14] With a pocket knife they chiseled wood out of the rafters and decorated the 144 domino-like tiles with signs drawn by a fellow-prisoner in her native Chinese.

For several months I took "Advanced English" from Ruth Russell-Roberts. She made sure my English sounded upper-class, and told me how to behave at hunts ("Call the red coats 'pink,' after a Mr. Pink, who designed them"), garden parties, horse races, cricket matches, the kind of events I had seen pictures of in the British society magazine *Tattler*. I felt I would fit right in if ever I attended one of those events when the war was over.

The concerts, teas, charades, lectures, and lessons all reflected the interests of the leisure-class women that most of us had been. These leisure activities kept us sane in the crushing boredom of internment, just as domestic skills—the womanly skills—kept us alive.

Ruth and I also met regularly at the end of the day to walk laps on Irenelaan. She was almost as tall as I, and in our identical camp costumes of shorts and halter top we looked alike, except for the straw boater hat Ruth wore on the back of her head even after the sun went down. The hat gave her a jaunty,[15] rakish[16] air and made her look too young to be the mother of the little girl she had sent from Singapore to England shortly after the Japanese invaded Malaya.

Ruth was very shy, and here, too, she and I were much alike. She talked little about her child, Lynette, but I gathered she was torn with worry. Was the girl safe in some English country village, far from the German air raids that must still be devastating London? And where was Ruth's husband, who had been serving in the British Army in Malaya? "If the Japanese would at least let us receive Red Cross messages," she said.

Shelagh was another of the English women I often walked with. We had both worked as secretaries in offices and had something to compare. She would tell me about what she called her "past sickness," her longing for lovely evenings when friends took her out.

"The boys looked so good in their mess kits. I felt nice in my evening dress and clean and lovely, and they appreciated my looking nice. And the little dinners we would have at home, and the tennis parties and all the fun—it is good to have had such good times so that we can remember them

---

14. **mah-jongg** game of Chinese origin that uses decorated tiles
15. **jaunty** smart or stylish
16. **rakish** dashing

. . . But, oh, to have someone to make a fuss over me here."

So we muddled along as a group, trying to make the best of it, to "count our blessings." Oh, there were chronic complainers, like the women Betty Jeffrey called "the hearts." They wailed about a heart condition that would prevent their participation in community chores. There were mothers who continuously bemoaned the absence of a local woman to take care of a child. In the Far East in those days it was not unusual for such a person to wake a child, bathe, dress, feed, tend him all day and put him to bed again. Now, suddenly, the mothers had to do all this. Some took their feelings of resentment out on the children. "Get out of the room, Jantje. I'm trying to roll up the beds so there'll be space for us to sit." "Don't shout, Muriel, I have a headache." "You horrible child, you got yourself dirty again, and I just washed your pants, and you know the water hasn't been turned on all day."

My sisters and I kept busy. Although we had entered the camp as a trio, and others spoke of us as "the three Colijn girls," we often saw each other only at meal times and during discussions about who was going to do what for our household. We now lived by rote. You do this today, I'll do it tomorrow.

As I befriended Shelagh and Ruth, Antoinette and Alette befriended members of the English singing groups and spent much time rehearsing for the latest show or songfest.

In addition, Antoinette was often trotting around doing something for someone else. Alette continued to mother little Wim and plod through *Les Misérables* with Sister Catharinia. I read through the library books.

We each sewed a dress from sarongs we had bought after the shipwreck. They were our "liberation dresses"—our "day-of-deliverance dresses," as some English called them—to wear when we would walk out of the camp. Mrs. van Zanen had shown us how to cut a pattern and sew pieces together by hand. Sewing, like cooking, had not yet been part of our education.

I also made a long-sleeved jacket out of gunny-sack material, open at the front and embroidered with cross stitching along the edges. The colors were red, white, and blue—the Dutch flag colors. I would have liked to add orange, the color of the banner flown along with the Dutch flag to honor the royal family of the House of Orange, but there was no orange thread in the camp. I was proud of my jacket.

Some Sundays I joined my sisters in English worship in Shelagh's garage, where her kongsi members had removed all bedrolls and pots and pans so they could have a service. It was often led by Miss Dryburgh. Her first name was Margaret, but I never called her that because of the age difference. She was in her early fifties.

When I first met Miss Dryburgh, she had struck me as a rather dull bird: eyes peering through thick round lenses, brownish hair in a tight bun at the back of her head, a short stocky figure wearing the sensible loose-fitting cotton dress and Mary Jane-type shoes she had worn on the *Mata-Hari* out of Singapore. But I soon discovered that Miss Dryburgh was not at all a dull woman.

I had already heard, that very first day in camp, part of her humorous "Palembang Camp Song" and watched a variety show she scripted. She also wrote little birthday poems and gallant tributes to those of us in camp. My sisters and I had been touched by her tribute to us:

> And when at length they take their place
> Within a world that needs brave youth,
> May past experience add new grace,
> Suffering give clearer view of truth,
> May life hold many blessings yet
> For Helen, Antoinette, Alette.

Apparently, she was good not only with poetry but with music as well. "She used to play the organ in our church in Singapore, in a great way," I was told. "She also taught fine piano to some of our youngsters."

In July 1942, Miss Dryburgh combined her poetic and musical talents and wrote the words and melody for "The Captives' Hymn."

"I was out flapping a fire when Miss Dryburgh thrust a piece of paper in my hands," Shelagh told me. "She said, 'We're singing this as an anthem. You have to practice it.' And it was very difficult to sing, really. The words meant a lot. It was difficult not to show emotion."

The hymn premiered on July 5, 1942, in the garage of house number 9. It was sung a cappella[17] by Shelagh Brown, Dorothy MacLeod and Margaret Dryburgh, who sang the alto part.

> Father, in captivity
> We would lift our prayer to Thee,
> Keep us ever in Thy love,
> Grant that daily we may prove
> Those who place their trust in Thee,
> More than conquerors may be.

---

17. **a cappella** without musical accompaniment

Give us patience to endure,
Keep our hearts serene and pure,
Grant us courage, charity,
Greater faith, humility,
Readiness to own Thy will,
Be we free or captive still.

For our country we would pray,
In this hour be Thou her stay,
Pride and selfishness forgive,
Teach her by Thy laws to live,
By Thy grace may all men see
That true greatness comes from Thee.

For our loved ones we would pray,
Be their guardian night and day,
From all dangers keep them free,
Banish all anxiety,
May they trust us to Thy care.
Know that Thou our pains doth share.

May the day of freedom dawn,
Peace and justice be reborn.
Grant that nations loving Thee
O'er the world may brothers be,
Cleansed by suffering, know rebirth,
See Thy kingdom come on earth.

I was as moved as Shelagh, but, like her, I didn't want to show it. At that time I viewed the hymn, particularly the fourth verse about the loved ones, in terms of the emotions it evoked in me—a tender, touching hymn. Now I see it as a statement by a generous, forgiving, and loving woman. She doesn't bother to say who the conquerors were—just as in the camp she never used the word Jap, and never such expressions as others threw out like "nasty little devils." She showed no bitterness or anger, only courage and hope that o'er the world nations may brothers be. Now I see Margaret Dryburgh's "Captives' Hymn" as an instrument of peace.

from

...*I never saw another butterfly...:*

Children's Drawings and Poems from Terezin Concentration Camp, 1942–1944

Edited by Hana Volavková

The poems and drawings selected here were created by Jewish children confined at the Terezin Concentration Camp in the former Czechoslovakia from 1942 through 1944. The poems reflect the children's thoughts, dreams, and fears. The poems are part of a permanent exhibition on display at the United States Holocaust Memorial Museum in Washington, D.C.

A Note from the United States Holocaust Memorial Museum

IN 1989, the State Jewish Museum in Prague entered into a cooperative agreement to loan the United States Holocaust Memorial Museum twenty-four original drawings and to permit the museum to make fifty facsimiles[1] of original works by the children of Terezin for display in an exhibit on children in the Holocaust. The children's exhibit, which includes artifacts from the concentration camp/ghetto at Terezin, is part of a permanent exhibition on display at the museum in Washington, D.C.

The United States Holocaust Memorial Museum is the national memorial to the victims of the Holocaust. Chartered by a unanimous act of Congress and built on federal land with private funds donated by the American people, the museum has three components: a museum to tell the story of the Holocaust, a memorial to its victims, and educational programs with a moral mission.

This unique institution is an educational and historical museum. The artifacts, films, photographs, and documents presented in the museum's permanent exhibition tell the story of the Holocaust, beginning with the Nazi assumption of power in 1933 and concluding with the resettlement of survivors in the United States and Israel. Among the museum's important artifacts are a rail car of the type used to transport Jews from Warsaw to Treblinka, a barracks from Birkenau, and a Danish fishing boat that was used to ferry Jews to safety in Sweden. Some of the most cherished artifacts to be found in the museum are twenty-four original artworks from Theresienstadt along with fifty handmade facsimiles of the originals. These works of art—remnants of the lives of the children who drew them—will form the core of a major exhibit on the fate of the over one million Jewish children murdered by the Nazis.

The museum is also an educational institution to be visited by schoolchildren traveling with their teachers and by children accompanied by their

---

1. **facsimiles** copies

parents. In addition to its permanent exhibition, the museum presents an exhibition especially designed for elementary-school students entitled "Remember the Children," which portrays the experience of children during the Holocaust.

The opening of the museum in April 1993 and these exhibits have provided the opportunity to present an expanded edition of *I Never Saw Another Butterfly*, the well-known collection of poems and drawings by the children in Terezin. . . .

The children of Terezin left a remarkable legacy in their poetry and art. No less remarkable were the teachers who defied camp rules to offer the children art therapy in the guise[2] of art lessons, to teach literature, and to organize poetry contests, recitations, and cultural programs in the girls' and boys' dormitories. One such teacher was Friedl Dicker-Brandeis. A former student of the Bauhaus in Weimar, Germany, she was an accomplished artist, designer, and teacher. When she was ordered to Terezin in December 1942, she conceived a mission for herself and brought what art materials she could to the camp.

Mrs. Dicker-Brandeis saw that the children of Terezin needed a form of artistic expression as a way to moderate the chaos of their lives. Drawing on her Bauhaus experience and available supplies—her hoarded materials, office forms, scrap paper, cardboard, wrapping paper—she provided excellent training in art fundamentals, studies of everyday objects, imaginative drawing, and complex still lifes, all the while freeing her students to reveal their feelings through their art.

One of her students, Raja Engländerová, recalled in her memoirs: "I remember Mrs. Brandeis as a tender, highly intelligent woman, who managed—for some hours every week—to create a fairy world for us in Terezin . . . a world that made us forget all the surrounding hardships that we were not spared despite our young ages."

In most cases, little is known about the children of Terezin. Camp records generally provided only dates of birth; arrival at Terezin; and departure, destination, and fate. Many of the works were unsigned and thus the names of their young creators are unknown.

"Art constantly challenges the process by which the individual person is reduced to anonymity," writes the Israeli novelist Aharon Appelfeld, himself a child survivor of the Holocaust. Through their artistic expressions, the voices of these children, each one unique and individual, reach us across the abyss of the greatest crime in human history, allow us to touch them, and restore our own humanity in doing so.

---

2. **guise** appearance

Franta Bass

Illness

Sadness, stillness in the room.
In the middle, a table and a bed.
In the bed, a feverish boy.
His mother sits next to him
with a little book.
She reads him his favorite story
and immediately, the fever subsides.

Room with a Bunkbed, by Erika Taussigová, 1944

Anonymous

A Letter to Daddy

Momma told me to write to you today,
but I had no time. New children arrived
with the latest transport, and
I had to play with them.

5   I didn't notice time pass.

I live better these days.
I sleep on my own mattress on the floor,
so I will not fall down.
At least I don't have much work to fix up my bed,

10 and in the morning I see the sky from my window.

I was coughing a bit, but I don't want to get sick,
for I am happy when I can run in the courtyard.
Tonight there will be a gathering
like the ones at Scout camp in the summer.

15 We will sing songs we know,
a girl will play the accordion.
I know you wonder how we fare here,
and you would surely like to be with us now.

And something else, Daddy. Come soon

20 and have a more cheerful face!
When you are unhappy, Momma is sad,
and then I miss the sparkle in her eyes.

Continued

You promised to bring me books
because, truly, I have nothing to read.
25   So please, come tomorrow, right before dusk.
I will surely be grateful for this.

Now I must stop. Momma sends you her love.
I will rejoice when I hear your footsteps
in the hall. Until you are with us again,
30   I send you my greetings and kisses.

Your faithful son.

Man with a Mustache, by Hanuš Klauber

Figures of Little Girls, by Jana Hellerová, 1942–1944

Pavel Friedmann # The Butterfly

The last, the very last,
So richly, brightly, dazzlingly yellow.
Perhaps if the sun's tears would sing
        against a white stone. . . .

Such, such a yellow
Is carried lightly 'way up high.
It went away I'm sure because it wished to
        kiss the world good-bye.

For seven weeks I've lived in here,
Penned up inside this ghetto.
But I have found what I love here.
The dandelions call to me
And the white chestnut branches in the court.
Only I never saw another butterfly.

That butterfly was the last one.
Butterflies don't live in here,
        in the ghetto.

Bird and Butterfly, Artist unknown

**M. Košek, H.
Löwy, Bachner**

The Little Mouse

A mouse sat upon a shelf,
Catching fleas in his coat of fur.
But he couldn't catch her—what chagrin!—
She'd hidden 'way inside his skin.
He turned and wriggled, knew no rest,
That flea was such a nasty pest!

His daddy came
And searched his coat.
He caught the flea and off he ran.
To cook her in the frying pan.
The little mouse cried, "Come and see!
For lunch we've got a nice, fat flea!"

Untitled, by Helena Schanzerová

Man on a Boat, by Elly Hellerová

Alena Synková | # To Olga

Listen!
The boat whistle has sounded now
And we must sail
Out toward an unknown port.

We'll sail a long, long way
And dreams will turn to truth.
Oh, how sweet the name Morocco!
Listen!
Now it's time.

The wind sings songs of far away,
Just look up to heaven
And think about the violets.

Listen!
Now it's time.

the children in Barracks L318 and L417, ages 10–16 years

On a Sunny Evening

On a purple, sun-shot evening
Under wide-flowering chestnut trees
Upon the threshold full of dust
Yesterday, today, the days are all like these.

Trees flower forth in beauty,
Lovely, too, their very wood all gnarled and old
That I am half afraid to peer
Into their crowns of green and gold.

The sun has made a veil of gold
So lovely that my body aches.
Above, the heavens shriek with blue
Convinced I've smiled by some mistake.
The world's abloom and seems to smile.
I want to fly but where, how high?
If in barbed wire, things can bloom
Why couldn't I? I will not die!

Garden, by Ruth Ĉehová 1943–1944